TRAIL
MIX

D0920147

This book is dedicated to my aunt Robin, a fearless outdoorswoman, lover of nature, and a passionate writer who left this world too soon, but will always be remembered for her spirit of adventure.

CONTENTS

INTRODUCTION

I grew up in New York City. Not in the suburbs, not near the city, but in the heart of midtown Manhattan on the eighth floor of an apartment building. Though most of my outdoor play was conducted on concrete, including in my school's recess yard, I was lucky enough to have access to Gramercy Park, a gated neighborhood park with girthy, burled, old trees, manicured rows of shrubs, and large swaths of bright green grass. The funny thing about that small slice of nature was the museum-like quality it had: You couldn't walk on the grass, and you couldn't climb the trees. (Literally, there were "Keep Off the Grass" signs posted, and a park superintendent who enforced the policy strictly.) Not easy rules for nature-starved, energy-filled kids to follow, but my neighborhood friends and I still frequented the park and made the most of it, making up imaginary games that were no doubt inspired by the relative primitiveness of this outdoor oasis on an island of concrete.

Fast forward 25 years, and my life since high school has been shrouded in nature. It was as if that little glimpse of it opened some door, and when I walked through it, I knew I would never come back. Wilderness, open space, and mountains as a backdrop for my life quickly became a priority. I spent my college years in Colorado, moved to Montana upon graduation, and have been living here ever since. And to this day, the great outdoors and the adventures that lie within it—hiking, biking, floating rivers, fishing, skiing, or even just sitting by a river—are my go-to therapy. Nature, whether it's experienced on a path just outside of town or on top of a mountain, is where I contemplate and recreate, and as cliché as it sounds, it's what fills my cup and makes me happy.

When I was approached by FalconGuides to curate quotes about the outdoors, I couldn't pass it up. See, it seems to me that, now more than ever, people need inspiration to fall in love with nature, or, for those who already have, maybe find reinforcement in why they love and need it and why it's important to protect it.

I now have kids of my own who are growing up surrounded by mountains and outdoor activities, with no knowledge of big city life. The funny thing is, I still have to pry them out of doors, away from screens. I try to point out the beauty that surrounds us, get them to inspect the wildflowers, to want to hike a little farther without a bribe, or to make it through a full day of skiing. I want them to know they always have the great outdoors to lean on for clarity, mental and physical health, and inspiration.

Without sounding like a "kids these days" curmudgeon, I worry about the younger screen-locked generations, those who barely look up from their phones, much less look longingly at a mountain they're dying to climb. I also worry about those who work too much, spend too much time indoors, in offices or cubicles, living without the release and sense of freedom that comes with doses of nature.

I hope this selection of quotes from literary masters, philosophers, armchair psychologists, environmentalists, comedians, adventurers, explorers, and the like serves as a gentle reminder of the overall universal message intended here: There's a wisdom in the outdoors, and it's worth tapping into it. The lessons we learn there, whether it's a leisurely stroll or a conquered mountain, can, without a doubt, lead to a more inspired, happy life.

—CORINNE GAFFNER GARCIA

ADVENTURE

Life is either a daring adventure or nothing.

—Helen Keller

The sea is dangerous and its storms terrible, but these obstacles have never been sufficient reason to remain ashore . . . unlike the mediocre, intrepid spirits seek victory over those things that seem impossible . . . it is with an iron will that they embark on the most daring of all endeavors . . . to meet the shadowy future without fear and conquer the unknown.

—FERDINAND MAGELLAN, PORTUGUESE EXPLORER

If you can find a path with no obstacles, it probably doesn't lead anywhere.

—FRANK A. CLARK, AMERICAN POLITICIAN

Mountains should be climbed with as little effort as possible and without desire.

—ROBERT M. PIRSIG, *ZEN AND THE ART OF MOTORCYCLE MAINTENANCE: AN INQUIRY INTO VALUES*

We have an unknown distance yet to run, an unknown river to explore. What falls there are, we know not; what rocks beset the channel, we know not; what walls ride over the river, we know not. Ah, well! we may conjecture many things.

—JOHN WESLEY POWELL

The very basic core of a man's living spirit is his passion for adventure.

—JON KRAKAUER, *INTO THE WILD*

Adventure is worthwhile in itself.

—AMELIA EARHART

Mountains are not fair or unfair,
they are just dangerous.

—REINHOLD MESSNER, ITALIAN MOUNTAINEER

A journey is a person in itself, no two are
alike. We find after years of struggle that
we do not take a trip, a trip takes us.

—JOHN STEINBECK, *TRAVELS WITH CHARLEY:
IN SEARCH OF AMERICA*

Do not follow where the path may lead.

Go instead where there is no path

and leave a trail.

—Ralph Waldo Emerson

Without the possibility of death,

adventure is not possible.

—Reinhold Messner, Italian Mountaineer

The mountain remains unmoved

at seeming defeat by the mist.

—Rabindranath Tagore, Bengali Poet,
Musician, Artist

There is always an adventure
waiting in the woods.

—KATELYN S. BOLDS, AMERICAN AUTHOR

**The journey of a thousand miles
begins with a single step.**

—LAO TZU

The long distance hiker, a breed set apart,
from the likes of the usual pack. He'll
shoulder his gear, be hittin' the trail;
long gone, long 'fore he'll be back.

—M. J. EBERHART, AMERICAN WRITER & AVID HIKER

I can't understand why men make all this fuss about Everest—it's only a mountain.

—Junko Tabei, First Woman to Climb Mount Everest

You cannot see the Grand Canyon in one view, as if it were a changeless spectacle from which a curtain might be lifted, but to see it you have to toil from month to month through its labyrinths.

—John Wesley Powell

When you see someone putting on his Big Boots, you can be pretty sure that an Adventure is going to happen.

—A. A. Milne, *Winnie-the-Pooh*

Until you step into the unknown, you
don't know what you're made of.

—Roy T. Bennett, *The Light in the Heart*

**While on top of Everest, I looked across
the valley towards the great peak Makalu
and mentally worked out a route about
how it could be climbed. It showed me
that even though I was standing on
top of the world, it wasn't the end of
everything. I was still looking beyond
to other interesting challenges.**

—Sir Edmund Hillary, New Zealand Mountaineer

Adventure: The pursuit of life.

—Jenny Radcliffe, Social Engineering Expert

The longest journey begins with a single step, not with the turn of an ignition key.

—Edward Abbey, *The Journey Home*

Look, when do the really interesting things happen? Not when you've brushed your teeth and put on your pyjamas and are cozy in bed. They happen when you are cold and uncomfortable and hungry and don't have a roof over your head for the night.

—Ellen Potter, *The Kneebone Boy*

Spontaneity is the best kind of adventure.

—ANONYMOUS

Never fear quarrels, but seek
hazardous adventures.

—ALEXANDRE DUMAS, *THE THREE MUSKETEERS*

There are two kinds of climbers, those
who climb because their heart sings when
they're in the mountains, and all the rest.

—ALEX LOWE, AMERICAN CLIMBER

When we allow ourselves to
explore, we discover destinations
that were never on our map.

— AMIE KAUFMAN, *UNEARTHED*

**The greatest danger in life is
not to take the adventure.**

—George Leigh Mallory, English Mountaineer

People don't take trips, trips take people.

—John Steinbeck, *Travels with Charley:
In Search of America*

If you want a blank spot on the map,
you gotta leave the map behind.

—Jon Krakauer

. . . Camping can be the greatest expression
of free will, personal independence, innate
ability, and resourcefulness possible today
in our industrialized, urbanized existence.

—Anne LaBastille, American Author & Ecologist

There can be no conquest to the man
who dwells in the narrow and small
environment of a groveling life, and
there can be no vision to the man the
horizon of whose vision is limited by
the bounds of self. But the great things
of the world, the great accomplishments
of the world, have been achieved by
men who had high ideals and who have
received great visions. The path is not
easy, the climbing is rugged and hard,
but the glory at the end is worthwhile.

—MATTHEW ALEXANDER HENSON,
FIRST AFRICAN-AMERICAN ARCTIC EXPLORER

Then one day, when you least expect
it, the great adventure finds you.

—EWAN MCGREGOR, ACTOR

Nothing adventured, nothing attained.

—PETER ALEXANDER MCWILLIAMS, AMERICAN AUTHOR

Between every two pines there is
a doorway to a new world.

—JOHN MUIR

It's a dangerous business, Frodo, going
out your door. You step onto the road,
and if you don't keep your feet, there's no
knowing where you might be swept off to.

—J. R. R. TOLKIEN, *THE FELLOWSHIP OF THE RING*

Mountain hikes instilled in me a
life-long urge to get to the top of
any inviting summit or peak.

—Paul D. Boyer, American Scientist

**Twenty years from now you will be more
disappointed by the things that you
didn't do than by the ones you did do. So
throw off the bowlines. Sail away from
the safe harbor. Catch the trade winds in
your sails. Explore. Dream. Discover.**

—H. Jackson Brown Jr., American Author

The big question is whether you are going to
be able to say a hearty yes to your adventure.

— Joseph Campbell, American Author

. . . Walk for glory or for adventure,
or to see new sights . . . and you will
very soon find how consonant is
walking with your whole being.

—HILAIRE BELLOC, ANGLO-FRENCH WRITER & HISTORIAN

**Boys should be allowed to climb tall
trees and walk along the tops of high
walls and dive into the sea from high
rocks . . . The same with girls. I like the
type of child who takes risks. Better by
far than the one who never does so.**

—ROALD DAHL, BRITISH AUTHOR

You are never going to climb anything
great if you don't take risks.

—JIMMY CHIN, AMERICAN MOUNTAINEER

So many glades; so little time.

—BILL MCKIBBEN, *WANDERING HOME: A LONG WALK ACROSS AMERICA'S MOST HOPEFUL LANDSCAPE*

Mount Everest, you beat me the first time, but I'll beat you the next time because you've grown all you are going to grow . . . but I'm still growing!

—SIR EDMUND HILLARY, NEW ZEALAND MOUNTAINEER

Only those who will risk going too far can possibly find out how far they can go.

—T. S. ELIOT

This life is yours. Take the power to choose what you want to do and do it well. Take the power to love what you want in life and love it honestly. Take the power to walk in the forest and be a part of nature. Take the power to control your own life. No one else can do it for you. Take the power to make your life happy.

—Susan Polis Schutz, American Poet

May your trails be crooked, winding,
lonesome, dangerous, leading to the
most amazing view. May your mountains
rise into and above the clouds.

—EDWARD ABBEY, *DESERT SOLITAIRE*

In overstepping our limitations, in
touching the extreme boundaries of
man's world, we have come to know
something of its true splendor.

—MAURICE HERZOG, FRENCH MOUNTAINEER

**Oh the things you can find,
if you don't stay behind!**

—DR. SEUSS

Half the charm of climbing mountains
is born in visions preceding this
experience—visions of what is
mysterious, remote, inaccessible.

—George Leigh Mallory, English Mountaineer

. . . Adventures aren't just about doing
something crazy, but rather about connecting
with forgotten core elements of life.

—Jellis Vaes, Artist

**Attitude is the difference between
an ordeal and an adventure.**

—Bob Bitchin, American Author & Adventurer

Adventure is worthwhile.

—Aesop

The wilderness and the idea of wilderness is one of the permanent homes of the human spirit.

—Joseph Wood Krutch, American Writer

Climb if you will, but remember that courage and strength are nought without prudence, and that a momentary negligence may destroy the happiness of a lifetime. Do nothing in haste; look well to each step; and from the beginning think what may be the end.

—Edward Whymper, *Scrambles Amongst the Alps*

Let your walks now be a little
more adventurous.

—HENRY DAVID THOREAU

Why do we travel to remote locations?
To prove our adventurous spirit or to
tell stories about incredible things? We
do it to be alone amongst friends and to
find ourselves in a land without man.

—GEORGE LEIGH MALLORY, *THE WILDEST DREAM:
THE BIOGRAPHY OF GEORGE MALLORY*
BY PETER GILLMAN AND LENI GILLMAN

**I have discovered that even the
mediocre can have adventures and
even the fearful can achieve.**

—SIR EDMUND HILLARY, NEW ZEALAND MOUNTAINEER

I take a fierce delight in swinging
a pack on my back or into a canoe
and heading for the hills or lakes.

—ANNE LABASTILLE, AMERICAN AUTHOR

Climbing is unadulterated hard labor.
The only real pleasure is the satisfaction
of going where no man has been
before and where few can follow.

—ANNIE SMITH PECK, AMERICAN MOUNTAINEER

You do not travel if you are afraid
of the unknown. You travel for the
unknown, that reveals you in yourself.

—ELLA MAILLART, SWISS ADVENTURER

It is still not hard to find a man who will adventure for the sake of a dream or one who will search, for the pleasure of searching, not for what he may find.

—Sir Edmund Hillary, New Zealand Mountaineer

You must go on adventures to find out where you truly belong.

—Sue Fitzmaurice, New Zealand Author

Life is brought down to the basics: if you are warm, regular, healthy, not thirsty or hungry, then you are not on a mountain . . .

—Chris Darwin, The Great-Great-Grandson of Charles Darwin

For me an adventure is something that I can take an active part in but that I don't have total control over.

—Peter Croft, Canadian Mountaineer

Walk into the woods. Keep walking. Walk off tracks. Do not plan where you are going. Take whatever directions appeal in the moment. Keep walking. When (without realizing) you are lost, look into the eyes of the dragon, then your adventure begins.

—Tom Waterkrag, "Chucking Out Agendas and Thriving Again"

Every man can transform the world from one of monotony and drabness to one of excitement and adventure.

—Irving Wallace

All life in the wilderness is so pleasant
that the temptation is to consider each
particular variety, while one is enjoying
it, as better than any other. A canoe trip
through the great forests, a trip with
a pack-train among the mountains, a
trip on snow-shoes through the silent,
mysterious fairy-land of the woods in
winter—each has its peculiar charm.

—THEODORE ROOSEVELT

There was nowhere to go but everywhere,
so just keep on rolling under the stars.

—JACK KEROUAC, ON THE ROAD

You need special shoes for hiking—
and a bit of a special soul as well.

—TERRI GUILLEMETS, AMERICAN AUTHOR

**The wonderful things in life are the
things you do, not the things you have.**

—REINHOLD MESSNER, ITALIAN MOUNTAINEER

A perfect gift for anyone that loves the
outdoors is to invite them on an adventure.

—BEN STOOKESBERRY, OUTDOOR ADVENTURER

When preparing to climb a
mountain—pack a light heart.

—Dan May

Our drive, our ruggedness, our
unquenchable optimism and zeal
and elan go back to the challenges
of the untrammeled wilderness.

—Harvey Broome, American lawyer,
Writer & Conservationist

**Jobs fill your pockets, but
adventures fill your soul.**

— Jaime Lyn Beatty, American Actor

I walked to mountains and
defeated them. That's all.

—Jerzy Kukuczka, Polish Climber

Adventure is allowing the unexpected to happen to you. Exploration is experiencing what you have not experienced before.

—RICHARD ALDINGTON, *DEATH OF A HERO*

I will find a way out or make one.

—ROBERT PEARY, AMERICAN EXPLORER

The experienced mountain climber is not intimidated by a mountain—he is inspired by it.

—WILLIAM ARTHUR WARD, AMERICAN AUTHOR

BEAUTY

Nature is painting for us, day after day,
pictures of infinite beauty.

—John Ruskin

I believe in beauty. I believe in stones
and water, air and soil, people and
their future and their fate.

—ANSEL ADAMS

To me, a lush carpet of pine needles
. . . is more welcome than the
most luxurious Persian rug.

—HELEN KELLER

I was standing on the highest mountain of them all, and round about beneath me was the whole hoop of the world. And while I stood there I saw more than I can tell and I understood more than I saw; for I was seeing in a sacred manner the shapes of all things in the spirit, and the shape of all shapes as they must live together like one being. And I saw that the sacred hoop of my people was one of many hoops that made one circle, wide as daylight and as starlight, and in the center grew one mighty flowering tree to shelter all children of one mother and one father. And I saw that it was holy.

—BLACK ELK

The sea, once it casts its spell, holds one in its net of wonder forever.

—Jacques Yves Cousteau, French Explorer

The only noise now was the rain, pattering softly with the magnificent indifference of nature for the tangled passions of humans.

—Sherwood Smith, American Writer

Our ability to perceive quality in nature begins, as in art, with the pretty. It expands through successive stages of the beautiful to values as yet uncaptured by language.

—Aldo Leopold, *A Sand County Almanac and Sketches Here and There*

Nature is the art of God.

—Dante

I am the lover of uncontained and immortal beauty. In the wilderness, I find something more dear and connate than in streets or villages. In the tranquil landscape, and especially in the distant line of the horizon, man beholds somewhat as beautiful as his own nature.

—Ralph Waldo Emerson

May you always walk in Beauty.

—Black Elk

How small we feel with our petty
ambitions and strivings in the presence
of the great elemental forces of Nature.

—ARTHUR CONAN DOYLE, *SHERLOCK HOLMES: THE
COMPLETE NOVELS AND STORIES, VOLUME I*

Nature was here a series of wonders,
and a fund of delight.

—DANIEL BOONE

This curious world we inhabit is more
wonderful than convenient; more
beautiful than it is useful; it is more to
be admired and enjoyed than used.

—HENRY DAVID THOREAU

The sap was rising in the pines. The willows and aspens were bursting out in young buds. Shrubs and vines were putting on fresh garbs of green. Crickets sang in the nights, and in the days all manner of creeping, crawling things rustled forth into the sun. Partridges and woodpeckers were booming and knocking in the forest. Squirrels were chattering, birds singing, and overhead honked the wild-fowl driving up from the south in cunning wedges that split the air.

—JACK LONDON, *CALL OF THE WILD*

I know a bank where the wild thyme blows,

Where oxlips and the nodding violet grows,

Quite over-canopied with luscious woodbine,

With sweet musk-roses and with eglantine.

—WILLIAM SHAKESPEARE, *A MIDSUMMER NIGHT'S DREAM*

**Weeds are flowers too, once
you get to know them.**

—EEYORE, FROM A. A. MILNE'S *WINNIE THE POOH*

The earth has music for those who listen.

—GEORGE SANTAYANA, PHILOSOPHER

All we have, it seems to me, is the
beauty of art and nature and life, and
the love which that beauty inspires.

—EDWARD ABBEY, *THE JOURNEY HOME*

Nature has wrought with a
bolder hand in America.

—NATHANIEL PARKER WILLIS, AMERICAN AUTHOR & POET

**The greatest wonder is that we can see
these trees and not wonder more.**

—RALPH WALDO EMERSON

Deep in their roots, all flowers keep the light.

—THEODORE ROETHKE, AMERICAN POET

The beauty and charm of the wilderness
are his for the asking, for the edges
of the wilderness lie close beside the
beaten roads of the present travel.

—THEODORE ROOSEVELT

The whole long day was a blaze of sunshine. The ghostly winter silence had given way to the great spring murmur of awakening life. This murmur arose from all the land, fraught with the joy of living. It came from the things that lived and moved again, things which had been as dead and which had not moved during the long months of frost.

—JACK LONDON, *CALL OF THE WILD*

There is no better designer than nature.

—ALEXANDER MCQUEEN, FASHION DESIGNER

There's a sunrise and a sunset every single day, and they're absolutely free. Don't miss so many of them.

—JO WALTON, *AMONG OTHERS*

Outside lies magic.

—JOHN STILGOE, HISTORIAN

Next we slid into the river and had a swim . . . Not a sound anywheres—perfectly still— just like the whole world was asleep, only sometimes the bullfrogs a-clattering, maybe.

—MARK TWAIN, *THE ADVENTURES OF HUCKLEBERRY FINN*

Nature never hurries. Atom by atom,
little by little, she achieves her work.

—RALPH WALDO EMERSON

**The first wildflower of the year
is like land after sea.**

—THOMAS WENTWORTH HIGGINSON, AMERICAN UNITARIAN
MINISTER, AUTHOR & ABOLITIONIST

And if these mountains had eyes, they
would wake to find two strangers in their
fences, standing in admiration as a breathing
red pours its tinge upon earth's shore.

—DONALD MILLER, *THROUGH PAINTED DESERTS:
LIGHT, GOD, AND BEAUTY ON THE OPEN ROAD*

The stars are forth, the moon above the tops

Of the snow-shining mountains. Beautiful!

I linger yet with Nature, for the night

Hath been to me a more familiar face

Than that of man; and in her starry shade

Of dim and solitary loveliness,

I learn'd the language of another world.

—LORD BYRON, "MANFRED"

The smell of wetted dust and wetted
sagebrush in a desert thundershower, is a
fragrance more packed with associations
than the most romantic of flowers.

—WALLACE STEGNER, *THE SOUND OF MOUNTAIN WATER*

The world of wonder is
wonderful wilderness.

—Lailah Gifty Akita, Ghanaian and founder of
Smart Youth Volunteers Foundation

Nature provides exceptions to every rule.

—Margaret Fuller, American Journalist

Finding beauty in a broken world is
creating beauty in the world we find.

—Terry Tempest Williams, "Terry Tempest Williams
on the Perspective of Nature and Healing," Interview
with Laurie Hertzel

Raindrops blossom brilliantly in the
rainbow, and change to flowers in the
sod, but snow comes in full flower
direct from the dark, frozen sky.

—John Muir, *The Mountains of California*

The sky is the daily bread of the eyes.

—RALPH WALDO EMERSON

With the aurora borealis flaming coldly overhead, or the stars leaping in the frost dance, and the land numb and frozen under its pall of snow, this song of the huskies might have been the defiance of life, only it was pitched in minor key, with long-drawn wailings and half-sobs, and was more the pleading of life, the articulate travail of existence.

—JACK LONDON, *CALL OF THE WILD*

I wonder if the snow loves the trees and fields, that it kisses them so gently? And then it covers them up snug, you know, with a white quilt; and perhaps it says, "Go to sleep, darlings, till the summer comes again."

—LEWIS CARROLL

To walk in nature is to witness a thousand miracles.

—MARY DAVIS, AUTHOR

Autumn is a second spring when every leaf is a flower.

—ALBERT CAMUS, *CALIGULA AND THREE OTHER PLAYS*

This is the most beautiful place on Earth. There are many such places.

—EDWARD ABBEY, *DESERT SOLITAIRE*

. . . and then, in dreaming, / The clouds methought would open and show riches / Ready to drop upon me, that when I waked / I cried to dream again.

—WILLIAM SHAKESPEARE, *THE TEMPEST*

Land forests are the coral reefs of the ocean of air.

—STEVEN MAGEE, *TOXIC ELECTRICITY*

Not just beautiful, though—the stars are like the trees in the forest, alive and breathing. And they're watching me.

—HARUKI MURAKAMI, *KAFKA ON THE SHORE*

How glorious a greeting the sun gives the mountains!

—JOHN MUIR

Nature always wears the colors of the spirit.

—Ralph Waldo Emerson

Inebriate of Air—am I—
And Debauchee of Dew—
Reeling—thro endless summer days—
From Inns of Molten Blue—"

—Emily Dickinson, *Selected Poems*

There are no words that can tell the hidden spirit of the wilderness, that can reveal its mystery, its melancholy, and its charm.

—Theodore Roosevelt

Those who contemplate the beauty
of the earth find reserves of strength
that will endure as long as life lasts.

—RACHEL CARSON, *SILENT SPRING*

The scientist does not study nature because
it is useful to do so. He studies it because he
takes pleasure in it, and he takes pleasure in
it because it is beautiful. If nature were not
beautiful it would not be worth knowing,
and life would not be worth living.

—HENRI POINCARÉ, *SCIENCE AND METHOD*

Nature is pleased with simplicity.
And nature is no dummy.

—SIR ISAAC NEWTON, ENGLISH MATHEMATICIAN,
PHYSICIST & ASTRONOMER

. . . so wondrous wild, the whole might
seem, the scenery of a fairy dream.

—Sir Walter Scott, "The Lady of the Lake"

I believe a leaf of grass is no less than
the journey-work of the stars.

—Walt Whitman, "Song of Myself"

Nothing is art if it does not
come from nature.

—Antoni Gaudi, Catalan Architect

**I had gained the summit of a commanding
ridge, and, looking round with
astonishing delight, beheld the ample
plains, the beauteous tracts below.**

—Daniel Boone

Nature is an infinite sphere of
which the center is everywhere and
the circumference nowhere.

—BLAISE PASCAL, FRENCH MATHEMATICIAN & PHYSICIST

Bees blew like cake-crumbs through
the golden air, white butterflies like
sugared wafers, and when it wasn't
raining a diamond dust took over which
veiled and yet magnified all things.

— LAURIE LEE, *CIDER WITH ROSIE*

**As I walk . . . as I walk . . . / The
universe . . . is walking with me . . .
/ Beautifully . . . it walks before me
. . . / Beautifully . . . on every side . . .
. / As I walk . . . I walk with beauty.**

—MARY HUNTER AUSTIN, AMERICAN WRITER

**Heaven is under our feet as
well as over our heads.**

—HENRY DAVID THOREAU, *WALDEN*

The diversity of the phenomena of
nature is so great, and the treasures
hidden in the skies so rich, precisely in
order that the human mind shall never
be lacking in fresh nourishment.

—JOHANNES KEPLER, GERMAN MATHEMATICIAN
& ASTRONOMER

Nothing could be more lonely and nothing
more beautiful than the view at nightfall
across the prairies to these huge hill masses,
when the lengthening shadows had at
last merged into one and the faint afterglow of the red sunset filled the west.

—THEODORE ROOSEVELT

There is nothing useless in nature;
not even uselessness itself.

—MONTAIGNE, FRENCH PHILOSOPHER

**In the hopes of reaching the
moon, men fail to see the flowers
that blossom at their feet.**

—ALBERT SCHWEITZER, ALSATIAN THEOLOGIAN

A flower's structure leads a bee toward
having pollen adhere to its body . . .
we don't know of any such reason why
beautiful places attract humans.

—DAVID RAINS WALLACE, *THE UNTAMED GARDEN AND
OTHER PERSONAL ESSAYS*

The poetry of the earth is never dead.

—JOHN KEATS, "ON THE GRASSHOPPER AND CRICKET"

Wilderness. The word itself is music.

—EDWARD ABBEY, *DESERT SOLITAIRE*

A summer rain had left the night clean
and sparkling with drops of water.

—ANNE RICE, *INTERVIEW WITH THE VAMPIRE*

Colors are the smiles of nature.

—LEIGH HUNT, ENGLISH POET

I think it annoys God if you walk by the
color purple in a field and don't notice.

—ALICE WALKER, *THE COLOR PURPLE*

It's the great, big, broad land 'way up yonder,
It's the forests where silence has lease; It's
the beauty that thrills me with wonder,
It's the stillness that fills me with peace.

—ROBERT W. SERVICE, BRITISH-CANADIAN POET & WRITER

**The creation of a thousand
forests is in one acorn.**

—RALPH WALDO EMERSON

I don't ask for the meaning of the song of a bird or the rising of the sun on a misty morning. There they are, and they are beautiful.

—PETE HAMILL, AMERICAN WRITER

How could this earth of ours, which is only a speck in the heavens, have so much variety of life, so many curious and exciting creatures?

—WALT DISNEY

Rain is grace; rain is the sky descending to earth; without rain, there would be no life.

—JOHN UPDIKE, *THE CENTAUR*

Every flower is a soul blossoming in nature.

—GERARD DE NERVAL, FRENCH WRITER

**In all things of nature there is
something of the marvelous.**

—ARISTOTLE

It was such a spring day as breathes
into a man an ineffable yearning, a
painful sweetness, a longing that makes
him stand motionless, looking at the
leaves or grass, and fling out his arms
to embrace he knows not what.

—JOHN GALSWORTHY, *THE FORSYTE SAGA*

All my life through, the new sights of
Nature made me rejoice like a child.

—MARIE CURIE

The earth laughs in flowers.

—Ralph Waldo Emerson

I think nature's imagination is so
much greater than man's, she's
never going to let us relax.

—Richard Phillips Feynman, Physicist

Nature is an outcry, unpolished truth; the
art—a euphemism—tamed wilderness.

—Dejan Stojanovic, Serbian Writer

**Many eyes go through the meadow,
but few see the flowers in it.**

—Ralph Waldo Emerson

To wake in that desert dawn was like
waking in the heart of an opal.

—GERTRUDE BELL, ENGLISH WRITER

**He was the owner of the moonlight on
the ground, he fell in love with the most
beautiful of the trees, he made wreaths of
leaves and strung them around his neck.**

—TOVE JANSSON, *TALES FROM MOOMINVALLEY*

They are beautiful, heart-rendingly beautiful,
those wilds, with a quality of wide-eyed,
unsung, innocent surrender that my
lacquered, toy-bright Swiss villages and
exhaustively lauded Alps no longer possess.

—VLADIMIR NABOKOV, *LOLITA*

**Everything holds its breath except spring.
She bursts through as strong as ever.**

—B. M. BOWER, AMERICAN WRITER

Some of nature's most exquisite
handiwork is on a miniature scale, as
anyone knows who has ever applied
a magnifying glass to a snowflake.

—RACHEL CARSON, *THE SENSE OF WONDER*

It's opener there in the wide open air.

—DR. SEUSS

Roll on, thou deep and dark blue Ocean—roll!

Ten thousand fleets sweep over thee in vain;

Man marks the earth with ruin—his control

Stops with the shore;—upon the watery plain

The wrecks are all thy deed, nor doth remain

A shadow of man's ravage, save his own,

When for a moment, like a drop of rain,

He sinks into thy depths with bubbling groan,

Without a grave, unknelled, uncoffined, and unknown.

His steps are not upon thy paths,—thy fields

Are not a spoil for him,—thou dost arise

And shake him from thee; the vile strength he wields

For earth's destruction thou dost all despise,

Spurning him from thy bosom to the skies,

And send'st him, shivering in thy playful spray

And howling, to his gods, where haply lies

His petty hope in some near port or bay,

And dashest him again to earth: —there let him lay.

—Lord Byron, "Childe Harold's Pilgrimage"

As a child, one has that magical capacity

to move among the many eras of the earth;

to see the land as an animal does . . .

—VALERIE ANDREWS, *A PASSION FOR THIS EARTH:*
EXPLORING A NEW PARTNERSHIP OF MAN,
WOMAN & NATURE

**In wilderness I sense the miracle
of life, and behind it our scientific
accomplishments fade to trivia.**

—CHARLES A. LINDBERGH, AMERICAN AVIATOR

The sunlight clasps the earth, and the
moonbeams kiss the sea: what are all these
kissings worth, if thou kiss not me?

—PERCY BYSSHE SHELLEY, "LOVE'S PHILOSOPHY"

Outside lies utterly ordinary space
open to any casual explorer willing
to find the extraordinary.

—JOHN STILGOE, HISTORIAN

There are some places so beautiful they can
make a grown man break down and weep.

—EDWARD ABBEY, *THE MONKEY WRENCH GANG*

The fairest thing in nature, a flower, still
has its roots in earth and manure.

—D. H. LAWRENCE, ENGLISH WRITER & POET

**Another glorious day, the air as delicious
to the lungs as nectar to the tongue.**

—JOHN MUIR

At some point in life the world's beauty becomes enough. You don't need to photograph, paint, or even remember it. It is enough.

—Toni Morrison, *Tar Baby*

There was music in the forest. There was clean air where nobody could hear him breathe.

—Daniel J. Rice, *This Side of a Wilderness*

Walk as if you are kissing the Earth with your feet.

—Thich Nhat Hanh, Zen Master

No spring nor summer beauty hath such grace as I have seen in one autumnal face.

—John Donne, "The Autumnal"

In the fairy's song the earth recognized
the names by which it called itself.

—SUSANNA CLARKE, *JONATHAN STRANGE & MR. NORRELL*

To the dull mind nature is leaden. To
the illumined mind the whole world
burns and sparkles with light.

—RALPH WALDO EMERSON

. . . the most distinctive, and perhaps
the most impressive, characteristic of
American scenery is its wildness.

—THOMAS COLE, PAINTER

CALL OF THE
WILD

The mountains are calling and I must go.

—John Muir

The love of wilderness is more than a
hunger for what is always beyond reach;
it is also an expression of loyalty to
the earth, the earth which bore us and
sustains us, the only paradise we shall
ever know, the only paradise we ever
need, if only we had the eyes to see.

—EDWARD ABBEY, *DESERT SOLITAIRE*

**You're off to great places! Today
is your day! Your mountain is
waiting, So get on your way!**

—DR. SEUSS

There are some who can live without
wild things and some who cannot.

—ALDO LEOPOLD

I could never resist the call of the trail.

—BUFFALO BILL CODY

Go outside. Don't tell anyone and don't bring your phone. Start walking and keep walking until you no longer know the road like the palm of your hand, because we walk the same roads day in and day out, to the bus and back home and we cease to see.

—CHARLOTTE ERIKSSON, SWEDISH WRITER

Why do you want to climb Mt. Everest? Because it is there.

—GEORGE LEIGH MALLORY, ENGLISH MOUNTAINEER, QUOTED IN *NEW YORK TIMES*, MARCH 18, 1923

Sometimes he pursued the call into the forest, looking for it as though it were a tangible thing, barking softly or defiantly . . . Irresistible impulses seized him. He would be lying in camp, dozing lazily in the heat of the day, when suddenly his head would lift and his ears cock up, intent and listening, and he would spring on his feet and dash away, and on and on, for hours, though the forest aisles.

—JACK LONDON, *CALL OF THE WILD*

I have seen the light in the wilderness and I must follow it.

—SETH ADAM SMITH, AMERICAN WRITER

Wilderness is not only a haven for native plants and animals but it is also a refuge from society. It's a place to go to hear the wind and little else, see the stars and the galaxies, smell the pine trees, feel the cold water, touch the sky and the ground at the same time, listen to coyotes, eat the fresh snow, walk across the desert sands, and realize why it's good to go outside of the city and the suburbs. Fortunately, there is wilderness just outside the limits of the cities and the suburbs in most of the United States, especially in the West.

—JOHN MUIR

The mountains were there and so was I.

—Maurice Herzog, French Mountaineer

Adventure should be 80 percent "I think this is manageable," but it's good to have that last 20 percent where you're right outside your comfort zone. Still safe, but outside your comfort zone.

—Bear Grylls, British Adventurer

But especially he loved to run in the dim twilight of the summer midnights, listening to the subdued and sleepy murmurs of the forest, reading signs and sounds as a man may read a book, and seeking for the mysterious something that called—called, waking or sleeping, at all times, for him to come.

—Jack London, *Call of the Wild*

Me thinks that the moment my legs begin
to move, my thoughts begin to flow.

—HENRY DAVID THOREAU

It had to do with how it felt

to be in the wild . . .

—CHERYL STRAYED, *WILD: FROM LOST TO FOUND
ON THE PACIFIC CREST TRAIL*

Challenge is what makes men. It
will be the end when men stop
looking for new challenges.

—SIR EDMUND HILLARY, NEW ZEALAND MOUNTAINEER

Who wouldn't be a Mountaineer! Up here
all the world's prizes seem nothing.

—JOHN MUIR

Every morning was a cheerful invitation
to make my life of equal simplicity, and I
may say innocence, with Nature herself.

—HENRY DAVID THOREAU

Wilds whisper, yet I long for their roar.

—GIN GETZ, *THE COLOR OF THE WILD*

Two roads diverged in a wood and I—
I took the one less traveled by, and
that has made all the difference.

—ROBERT FROST, "THE ROAD NOT TAKEN"

Late in August the lure of the
mountains becomes irresistible.

—EDWARD ABBEY, *DESERT SOLITAIRE*

. . . returning to nature has been a dream present in the minds of every generation since mankind first left nature.

—DANIEL J. RICE, *THE UNPEOPLED SEASON: JOURNAL FROM A NORTH COUNTRY WILDERNESS*

I was surprised, as always, by how easy the act of leaving was, and how good it felt. The world was suddenly rich with possibility.

—JACK KEROUAC, *ON THE ROAD*

To a person sitting quietly at home, Rocky Mountain traveling, like Rocky Mountain scenery, must seem very monotonous; but not so to me, to whom the pure, dry mountain air is the elixir of life.

—ISABELLA BIRD, ENGLISH EXPLORER

Nature is not a place to visit. It is home.

—GARY SNYDER, AMERICAN POET & ACTIVIST

Whenever the sun is shining, I feel obligated to play outside!

—CHARLES M. SCHULZ, *THE COMPLETE PEANUTS, VOL. 1: 1950–1952*

There is language going on out there— the language of the wild. Roars, snorts, trumpets, squeals, whoops, and chirps all have meaning derived over eons of expression . . .We have yet to become fluent in the language—and music—of the wild.

—BOYD NORTON, *SERENGETI: THE ETERNAL BEGINNING*

Oftentimes, it's only when we are in the wilds, amidst nature, when we are challenged to reconnect with our main primal needs.

—JELLIS VAES, ARTIST & ADVENTURER

Afoot and lighthearted I take to the open road, healthy, free, the world before me.

—WALT WHITMAN

Despite all I have seen and experienced, I still get the same thrill out of glimpsing a tiny patch of snow in a high mountain gully and feel the same urge to climb toward it.

—SIR EDMUND HILLARY, NEW ZEALAND MOUNTAINEER

There's a land—oh, it beckons and beckons. And I want to go back—and I will.

—ROBERT W. SERVICE, BRITISH-CANADIAN POET

I went to the woods because I wished
to live deliberately, to front only the
essential facts of life, and see if I could
not learn what it had to teach, and not,
when I came to die, discover that I had
not lived. I did not wish to live what was
not life, living is so dear; nor did I wish
to practise resignation, unless it was
quite necessary. I wanted to live deep and
suck out all the marrow of life, to live so
sturdily and Spartan-like as to put to rout
all that was not life, to cut a broad swath
and shave close, to drive life into a corner,
and reduce it to its lowest terms . . .

—Henry David Thoreau, *Walden*

She should be on a hill somewhere, under a fruit tree, with the sun and clouds above her and the rain to wash her clean.

—George R. R. Martin, *A Game of Thrones*

The appeal of the wild for me is its unpredictability. You have to develop an awareness, react fast, be resourceful and come up with a plan and act on it.

—Bear Grylls, British Adventurer

I am losing precious days. I am degenerating into a machine for making money. I am learning nothing in this trivial world of men. I must break away and get out into the mountains to learn the news.

—John Muir

Go for a walk outdoors. Reconnect with the feeling of the wind blowing through your hair. Listen to the birds that live in a tree in your yard. Watch the sunset.

—SKYE ALEXANDER, *THE MODERN GUIDE TO WITCHCRAFT*

I was disoriented by the idea that men should ever leave the forest.

—DANIEL J. RICE, *THE UNPEOPLED SEASON: JOURNAL FROM A NORTH COUNTRY WILDERNESS*

Let's not mince words: Everest doesn't attract a whole lot of well-balanced folks.

—JON KRAKAUER

In our forests

part divine

and makes her heart palpitate

wild and tame are one. What

a delicious Sound!

—JOHN CAGE, *M: WRITINGS '67–'72*

Beyond the wall of the unreal city . . .

there is another world waiting for you.

—EDWARD ABBEY, *BEYOND THE WALL:
ESSAYS FROM THE OUTSIDE*

**I see my path, but I don't know where
it leads. Not knowing where I'm going
is what inspires me to travel it.**

—ROSALIA DE CASTRO, SPANISH WRITER

**Study nature, love nature, stay close
to nature. It will never fail you.**

—MONET

No single mountain ever came to
me . . . so I always go to them.

—ERIK TANGHE, ARTIST

A person does not grow from the ground
like a vine or a tree, one is not part of a plot
of land. Mankind has legs so it can wander.

—ROMAN PAYNE, *THE WANDRESS*

Thousands of tired, nerve-shaken, over-
civilized people are beginning to find
out that going to the mountains is going
home; that wildness is a necessity; and
that mountain parks and reservations are
useful not only as fountains of timber and
irrigating rivers, but as fountains of life.

—JOHN MUIR

The earth has its music for
those who will listen.

—GEORGE SANTAYANA, PHILOSOPHER

Wildness reminds us what it means to
be human, what we are connected to
rather than what we are separate from.

—TERRY TEMPEST WILLIAMS, *RED: PASSION
AND PATIENCE IN THE DESERT*

Because in the end, you won't
remember the time you spent working
in the office or mowing your lawn.
Climb that goddamn mountain.

—JACK KEROUAC, *THE DHARMA BUMS*

The time to prepare for your next
expedition is when you have just
returned from a successful trip.

—ROBERT PEARY, AMERICAN EXPLORER

All good things are wild and free.

—HENRY DAVID THOREAU

More and more people seem to be separating
from nature. I'm trying to go in a different
direction. I'm getting closer and closer.

—DEAN POTTER, AMERICAN CLIMBER

Under the greenwood tree,

Who loves to lie with me

And tune his merry note,

Unto the sweet bird's throat;

Come hither, come hither, come hither.

Here shall he see

No enemy

But winter and rough weather.

—WILLIAM SHAKESPEARE, *As You Like It*

The mountains knew the definition of freedom. They provided a place where he could find his mind.

—DANIEL J. RICE, *This Side of a Wilderness*

We like the taste of freedom . . .

because we like the smell of danger.

—EDWARD ABBEY, *Beyond the Wall: Essays from the Outside*

I want to solve a climbing problem in the mountains, not in the sporting goods store.

—Reinhold Messner, Italian Mountaineer

Of all the paths you take in life, make sure a few of them are dirt.

—John Muir

If you wish to know the divine, feel the wind on your face and the warm sun on your hand.

—Eido Tai Shimano Roshi, Zen Buddhist Teacher

For me, it always comes back to the land . . . This is the source of where my power lies, the source of where all our power lies.

—Terry Tempest Williams

To be admitted to Nature's hearth costs nothing. None is excluded, but excludes himself. You have only to push aside the curtain.

—Henry David Thoreau

That's what mountains do, they taunt you, lure you to the freedom of the wilderness . . .

—Shannon M. Mullen, *See What Flowers*

Leave the road, take the trails.

—Pythagoras

Deep in the forest a call was sounding, and
as often as he heard this call, mysteriously
thrilling and luring, he felt compelled to
turn his back upon the fire and the beaten
earth around it, and to plunge into the forest,
and on and on, he knew not where or why;
nor did he wonder where or why, the call
sounding imperiously, deep in the forest.

—JACK LONDON, *CALL OF THE WILD*

I don't deny that there can be an element
of escapism in mountaineering, but
this should never overshadow its real
essence, which is not escape but victory
over your own human frailty.

—WALTER BONATTI, ITALIAN MOUNTAINEER

To be in touch with wilderness is to
have stepped past the proud cattle
of the field and wandered far from
the twinkles of the Inn's fire.

—Martin Shaw, English Actor

**I believe it is in our nature to explore, to
reach out into the unknown. The only true
failure would be not to explore at all.**

—Ernest Shackleton, British Explorer

Some of us are drawn to mountains the
way the moon draws the tide. Both the
great forests and the mountains live in
my bones. They have taught me, humbled
me, purified me and changed me.

—Joan Halifax, *The Fruitful Darkness: A Journey
Through Buddhist Practice and Tribal Wisdom*

**I wish I were out of doors! I wish
I were a girl again, half savage
and hardy, and free . . .**

— EMILY BRONTË, *WUTHERING HEIGHTS*

There is a love of wild nature in everybody,
an ancient mother-love showing
itself whether recognized or no, and
however covered by cares and duties.

—JOHN MUIR

Great things are done when men
and mountains meet; this is not
done by jostling in the street.

— WILLIAM BLAKE, *NOTEBOOKS*

The most difficult part of any endeavour is taking the first step, making the first decision.

—ROBYN DAVIDSON, AUSTRALIAN WRITER

Outdoors is our element: the exact sensation of living there.

—FRÉDÉRIC GROS, *A PHILOSOPHY OF WALKING*

We simply need that wild country available to us, even if we never do more than drive to its edge and look in.

—WALLACE STEGNER, *CROSSING TO SAFETY*

He was sounding the deeps of his nature, and
of the parts of his nature that were deeper
than he, going back into the womb of Time.

—JACK LONDON, *CALL OF THE WILD*

**I love to escape to wild places—forests,
mountains, rivers or the sea.**

—JANE WILSON-HOWARTH, BRITISH PHYSICIAN

Hiking's not for everyone. Notice
the wilderness is mostly empty.

—SONJA YOERG, *THE MIDDLE OF SOMEWHERE*

. . . nothing is more damaging to the adventurous spirit within a man than a secure future.

—JON KRAKAUER, *INTO THE WILD*

I need this wild life, this freedom.

—ZANE GREY, *THE VANISHING AMERICAN*

During all these years there existed within me a tendency to follow Nature in her walks.

—JOHN JAMES AUDUBON

If we were meant to stay in one place, we'd have roots instead of feet.

—RACHEL WOLCHIN, AMERICAN WRITER

Dust if you must, but there's not much time,

With rivers to swim, and mountains to climb.

—ROSE MILLIGAN, "DUST IF YOU MUST"

**The clearest way into the universe
is through a forest wilderness.**

—JOHN MUIR

CONSERVATION

The idea of wilderness needs no defense.
It only needs more defenders.

—EDWARD ABBEY, *THE JOURNEY HOME*

**Take nothing but memories,
leave nothing but footprints!**

—CHIEF SEATTLE

Nature does nothing uselessly.

—ARISTOTLE

And to lose the chance to see frigatebirds
soaring in circles above the storm, or a file
of pelicans winging their way homeward
across the crimson afterglow of the
sunset, or a myriad terns flashing in the
bright light of midday as they hover in
a shifting maze above the beach—why,
the loss is like the loss of a gallery of the
masterpieces of the artists of old time.

—THEODORE ROOSEVELT

If you know wilderness in the way that you know love, you would be unwilling to let it go.

— TERRY TEMPEST WILLIAMS, *RED: PASSION AND PATIENCE IN THE DESERT*

I think people who don't know the woods very well sometimes imagine it as a kind of undifferentiated mass of greenery, an endless continuation of the wall of trees they see lining the road.

—BILL MCKIBBEN, *WANDERING HOME: A LONG WALK ACROSS AMERICA'S MOST HOPEFUL LANDSCAPE*

People today have forgotten they're really just a part of nature. Yet, they destroy the nature on which our lives depend.

—AKIRA KUROSAWA, *YUME*

There is no separation between the health of human beings and the health of the land.

—TERRY TEMPEST WILLIAMS, *VOICE IN THE WILDERNESS: CONVERSATIONS WITH TERRY TEMPEST WILLIAMS*

We kill all the caterpillars, then complain there are no butterflies.

—JOHN MARSDEN, *THE DEAD OF NIGHT*

A world without lions and tigers and vultures and snakes and elk and bison would be—will be—a human zoo.

—EDWARD ABBEY, *POSTCARDS FROM ED: DISPATCHES AND SALVOS FROM AN AMERICAN ICONOCLAST*

Only when the last tree has been cut down,

Only when the last river has been poisoned,

Only when the last fish has been caught,

Only then will you find that

money cannot be eaten.

—CREE INDIAN PROPHECY

At one time in the world there were

woods that no one owned.

—CORMAC MCCARTHY, *CHILD OF GOD*

Love the world as your own self; then

you can truly care for all things.

—LAO TZU

If a man walks in the woods for love of them half of each day, he is in danger of being regarded as a loafer. But if he spends his days as a speculator, shearing off those woods and making the earth bald before her time, he is deemed an industrious and enterprising citizen.

—Henry David Thoreau

God wants His people to be a voice in the wilderness.

—Sunday Adelaja, Pastor

The care of the Earth is our most ancient and most worthy, and after all our most pleasing responsibility.

—Wendell Berry, *The Art of the Commonplace: The Agrarian Essays*

Man is the most insane species. He worships an invisible God and destroys a visible Nature. Unaware that this Nature he's destroying is this God he's worshiping.

—HUBERT REEVES, FRENCH CANADIAN ASTROPHYSICIST

If wilderness is outlawed, only outlaws can save wilderness.

—EDWARD ABBEY, *A VOICE CRYING IN THE WILDERNESS (VOX CLAMANTIS IN DESERTO): NOTES FROM A SECRET JOURNAL*

I am glad I shall never be young without wild country to be young in.

—ALDO LEOPOLD, *A SAND COUNTY ALMANAC AND SKETCHES HERE AND THERE*

Wildness is the preservation of the World.

—HENRY DAVID THOREAU, *WALKING*

The earth is what we all have in common.

—WENDELL BERRY

Nature is not our enemy, to be raped
and conquered. Nature is ourselves,
to be cherished and explored.

—TERENCE MCKENNA, AMERICAN ETHNOBOTANIST

The use of sea and air is common to all;
neither can a title to the ocean belong to
any people or private persons, forasmuch
as neither nature nor public use and
custom permit any possession thereof.

—QUEEN ELIZABETH I, *LETTERS*

To see ten thousand animals untamed
and not branded with the symbols of
human commerce is like scaling an
unconquered mountain for the first time,
or like finding a forest without roads or
footpaths, or the blemish of an axe.

—BERYL MARKHAM, *WEST WITH THE NIGHT*

**If you take away all the prairie dogs,
there will be no one to cry for the rain.**

—TERRY TEMPEST WILLIAMS

The land was not something to be feared
or conquered, and "wildlife" were neither
wild nor alien; they were relatives.

—DOUG PEACOCK, *GRIZZLY YEARS: IN SEARCH OF
THE AMERICAN WILDERNESS*

Wherever forests have not been mowed down, wherever the animal is recessed in their quiet protection, wherever the earth is not bereft of four-footed life—that to the white man is an "unbroken wilderness."

But for us there was no wilderness, nature was not dangerous but hospitable, not forbidding but friendly. Our faith sought the harmony of man with his surroundings; the other sought the dominance of surroundings.

For us, the world was full of beauty; for the other, it was a place to be endured until he went to another world.

But we were wise. We knew that man's heart, away from nature, becomes hard.

—Chief Luther Standing Bear

I am not an atheist but an earthiest. Be true to the earth.

—EDWARD ABBEY, *DESERT SOLITAIRE*

Earth is the holiest place in the Universe, loving the earth, and loving life is the way to generate positive vibrations.

—AMIT RAY, INDIAN SPIRITUAL MASTER

The soil under the grass is dreaming of a young forest, and under the pavement the soil is dreaming of grass.

—WENDELL BERRY, *GIVEN*

Here is your country. Cherish these natural wonders, cherish the natural resources, cherish the history and romance as a sacred heritage, for your children and your children's children.

—THEODORE ROOSEVELT

For most of history, man has had to fight nature to survive; in this century he is beginning to realize that, in order to survive, he must protect it.

—JACQUES-YVES COUSTEAU, FRENCH EXPLORER

What we called "wilderness" was to the Indian a homeland, "abiding loveliness" in Salish or Piegan.

—DOUG PEACOCK, *GRIZZLY YEARS: IN SEARCH OF THE AMERICAN WILDERNESS*

I think it is far more important to
save one square mile of wilderness,
anywhere, by any means, than to
produce another book on the subject.

—EDWARD ABBEY, *POSTCARDS FROM ED: DISPATCHES AND
SALVOS FROM AN AMERICAN ICONOCLAST*

**Daily prayers are delivered on the lips
of breaking waves, the whisperings of
grasses, the shimmering of leaves.**

—TERRY TEMPEST WILLIAMS

We shall never achieve harmony with
the land, anymore than we shall achieve
absolute justice or liberty for people.

—ALDO LEOPOLD, *ROUND RIVER: FROM THE
JOURNALS OF ALDO LEOPOLD*

Every green natural place we save saves a fragment of our sanity and gives us a little more hope that we have a future.

—WALLACE STEGNER

All America lies at the end of the wilderness road, and our past is not a dead past, but still lives in us.

—T. K. WHIPPLE, *STUDY OUT THE LAND: ESSAYS BY T. K. WHIPPLE*

The world owes you nothing. It was here first.

—MARK TWAIN

What would the world be, once bereft / Of wet and of wildness? Let them be left, / O let them be left, wildness and wet; / Long live the weeds and the wilderness yet.

—GERARD MANLEY HOPKINS, ENGLISH POET

What I stand for is what I stand on.

—WENDELL BERRY

What we are doing to the forests of the world is but a mirror reflection of what we are doing to ourselves and to one another.

—CHRIS MASER, *FOREST PRIMEVAL: THE NATURAL HISTORY OF AN ANCIENT FOREST*

Wilderness is not a luxury but a necessity of the human spirit, and as vital to our lives as water and good bread.

—EDWARD ABBEY, *DESERT SOLITAIRE*

Let us leave a splendid legacy for our
children . . . let us turn to them and
say, this you inherit: guard it well, for
it is far more precious than money . . .
and once destroyed, nature's beauty
cannot be repurchased at any price.

—ANSEL ADAMS

When the soil disappears,
the soul disappears.

—TERRI GUILLEMETS, AMERICAN WRITER

**Leave nothing but footprints; take nothing
but pictures; kill nothing but time.**

—JOHN KAY, SINGER/SONGWRITER

We can try to kill all that is native, string it up by its hind legs for all to see, but spirit howls and wildness endures.

—TERRY TEMPEST WILLIAMS, *AN UNSPOKEN HUNGER*

If we surrendered to earth's intelligence we could rise up rooted, like trees.

—RAINER MARIA RILKE, *RILKE'S BOOK OF HOURS: LOVE POEMS TO GOD*

When we see land as a community to which we belong, we may begin to use it with love and respect.

—ALDO LEOPOLD, *A SAND COUNTY ALMANAC*

The earth, like the sun, like the air, belongs to everyone—and to no one.

—EDWARD ABBEY, *THE JOURNEY HOME*

Do unto those downstream as you would have those upstream do unto you.

—Wendell Berry

Earth and sky, woods and fields, lakes and rivers, the mountain and the sea, are excellent schoolmasters, and teach of us more than we can ever learn from books.

—John Lubbock, *The Use of Life*

We do not inherit the earth from our ancestors; we borrow it from our children.

—Chief Seattle

Honoring a life is honoring the wide open space of wilderness and unknowing where the sacred dwells.

—Shannon Huffman Polson, *North of Hope: A Daughter's Arctic Journey*

**A forest is not a wilderness, but
a community of souls who speak
to one another on the wind.**

—ANTHONY T. HINCKS, AUTHOR

Nature, to be controlled, must be obeyed.

—FRANCIS BACON

It's amazing how quickly nature
consumes human places after we
turn our backs on them.

—SCOTT WESTERFELD, *IMPOSTERS*

A world without huge regions of total
wilderness would be a cage . . .

—EDWARD ABBEY, *POSTCARDS FROM ED: DISPATCHES AND
SALVOS FROM AN AMERICAN ICONOCLAST*

Something will have gone out of us as
a people if we ever let the remaining
wilderness be destroyed.

—WALLACE STEGNER, EXCERPT FROM A LETTER

Wilderness is the one kind of playground
which mankind cannot build to order . . .

—ALDO LEOPOLD, *A SAND COUNTY ALMANAC*

. . . We do not own these
woods. They own us.

—TIMOTHY GOODWIN, *WITHIN THESE WOODS: A
COLLECTION OF NORTHWOODS NATURE ESSAYS*

**Real freedom lies in wildness
not in civilization.**

—CHARLES LINDBERGH, AMERICAN AVIATOR

**I think having land and not ruining
it is the most beautiful art that
anybody could ever want.**

— ANDY WARHOL

. . . What occurs in nature, comes by
the hand of nature, and if the gods did
not approve, it would not be there.

—MERCEDES LACKEY, *MAGIC'S PAWN*

For myself I hold no preferences
among flowers, so long as they
are wild, free, spontaneous.

—EDWARD ABBEY, *DESERT SOLITAIRE*

Nature never did betray the
heart that loved her.

—William Wordsworth, "Lines Written a Few Miles
above Tintern Abbey"

To protect what is wild is to protect what
is gentle . . . Wild mercy is in our hands.

—Terry Tempest Williams, *Red: Passion and Patience in
the Desert*

**I would feel more optimistic about a
bright future for man if he spent less
time proving that he can outwit Nature
and more time tasting her sweetness
and respecting her seniority.**

—E. B. White, *Letters of E. B. White*

HAPPINESS

In the presence of nature, a wild delight runs
through the man, in spite of real sorrows.

—Ralph Waldo Emerson

It's wonderful to be back. Back among
the mountains that remind us of
our vulnerability, our ultimate lack
of control over the world we live in.
Mountains that demand humility, and
yield so much peace in return.

—ALEX LOWE, AMERICAN CLIMBER

I'd forgotten how enlivening it could
feel, seeing clearly and far. Aridity frees
light. It also unleashes grandeur.

—JULENE BAIR, *THE OGALLALA ROAD: A MEMOIR
OF LOVE AND RECKONING*

I just love any place that I can sit in the
sun and feel the warmth of the sun's rays,
and feel the connection to the planet . . .

—DEAN POTTER, AMERICAN CLIMBER

Life sucks a lot less when you add mountain air, a campfire and some peace and quiet.

—BROOKE HAMPTON, AUTHOR

Everything you can imagine, nature has already created.

—ALBERT EINSTEIN

May your trails be dim, lonesome, stony, narrow, winding and only slightly uphill.

—EDWARD ABBEY, *BEYOND THE WALL: ESSAYS FROM THE OUTSIDE*

He who climbs upon the highest mountains laughs at all tragedies, real or imaginary.

—FRIEDRICH NIETZSCHE

I laid there in the grass and the cool shade
thinking about things, and feeling rested
and ruther comfortable and satisfied. I
could see the sun out at one or two holes,
but mostly it was big trees all about, and
gloomy in there amongst them. There
was freckled places on the ground where
the light sifted down through the leaves,
and the freckled places swapped about
a little, showing there was a little breeze
up there. A couple of squirrels set on a
limb and jabbered at me very friendly.

—MARK TWAIN, *THE ADVENTURES OF HUCKLEBERRY FINN*

When you do something noble and beautiful and nobody noticed, do not be sad. For the sun every morning is a beautiful spectacle and yet most of the audience still sleeps.

—John Lennon

I am in love with this world . . . I have tilled its soil, I have gathered its harvest, I have waited upon its seasons, and always have I reaped what I have sown. I have climbed its mountains, roamed its forests, sailed its waters, crossed its deserts, felt the sting of its frosts, the oppression of its heats, the drench of its rains, the fury of its winds, and always have beauty and joy waited upon my goings and comings.

—John Burroughs, *The Summit of the Years*

If I fished only to capture fish, my fishing
trips would have ended long ago.

—ZANE GREY, *TALES OF SOUTHERN RIVERS*

It is wilderness that gets into your
nostrils, that runs with your sweat.
It is the core of everything living,
wilderness like molten iron.

—CRAIG CHILDS, *THE ANIMAL DIALOGUES: UNCOMMON
ENCOUNTERS IN THE WILD*

**We had no choice. Sadness was a
dangerous as panthers and bears. The
wilderness needs your whole attention.**

—LAURA INGALLS WILDER

A man on foot, on horseback or on a bicycle will see more, feel more, enjoy more in one mile than the motorized tourists can in a hundred miles.

—EDWARD ABBEY, *DESERT SOLITAIRE*

What we get from this adventure is just sheer joy. And joy is, after all, the end of life. We do not live to eat and make money.

—GEORGE LEIGH MALLORY, ENGLISH MOUNTAINEER

Happiness is the struggle towards a summit and, when it is attained, it is happiness to glimpse new summits on the other side.

—FRIDTJOF NANSEN, NORWEGIAN EXPLORER

To me, heaven on earth is
exploring on a trail.

—Deena Michelle Kastor, American Long-Distance
Runner

**"The best thing about hunting and fishing,"
the Old Man said, "is that you don't have
to actually do it to enjoy it. You can go
to bed every night thinking about how
much fun you had twenty years ago, and
it all comes back clear as moonlight."**

—Robert Ruark, "The Old Man's Boy Grows Older"

That's the thing about Mother
Nature, she really doesn't care what
economic bracket you're in.

—Whoopi Goldberg

I took a walk in the woods and
came out taller than the trees.

—HENRY DAVID THOREAU

Any woman who does not thoroughly enjoy
tramping across the country on a clear
frosty morning with a good gun and a pair
of dogs does not know how to enjoy life.

—ANNIE OAKLEY

**Everyone wants to live on top of the
mountain, but all the happiness and
growth occurs while you are climbing it.**

—ANDY ROONEY

I can testify that the best and maybe only
antidote for melancholia is action.

—EDWARD ABBEY, *A VOICE CRYING IN THE WILDERNESS
(VOX CLAMANTIS IN DESERTO)*

A vigorous five-mile walk will do more good for an unhappy but otherwise healthy adult than all the medicine and psychology in the world.

—PAUL DUDLEY WHITE, AMERICAN PHYSICIAN

So in two seconds away we went a-sliding down the river, and it did seem so good to be free again and all by ourselves on the big river, and nobody to bother us.

—MARK TWAIN, *THE ADVENTURES OF HUCKLEBERRY FINN*

I walked slowly to enjoy this freedom, and when I came out of the mountains, I saw the sky over the prairie . . .

—DANIEL J. RICE, *THE UNPEOPLED SEASON: JOURNAL FROM A NORTH COUNTRY WILDERNESS*

Just to lie here in the sun with great white peaks all around me and the biggest glacier in Europe at my feet, to eat from time to time, to sleep a little and dream a great deal—it is a heavenly existence.

—George Leigh Mallory, English Mountaineer

On the blue summer evenings, I will go along the paths, And walk over the short grass, as I am pricked by the wheat: Daydreaming I will feel the coolness on my feet.

—Arthur Rimbaud, "Sensation"

I felt my lungs inflate with the onrush of scenery—air, mountains, trees, people. I thought: This is what it is to be happy.

—Sylvia Plath, *The Bell Jar*

The happiness of the bee and the dolphin is to exist. For man it is to know that and to wonder at it.

—Jacques Yves Cousteau, French Explorer

Just walk, see, sit down if you like. And be. Just be, whatever you are with whatever you have, and realise that that is enough to be happy.

—Charlotte Eriksson, Author

That's the best thing about walking, the journey itself.

—Edward Abbey, *The Journey Home*

Joys come from simple and natural things;
mist over meadows, sunlight on leaves, the
path of the moon over water. Even rain
and wind and stormy clouds bring joy.

—Sigurd F. Olson, *The Singing Wilderness*

I never for a day gave up listening to
the songs of our birds, or watching
their peculiar habits, or delineating
them in the best way I could.

—John James Audubon

**Nobody climbs mountains for
scientific reasons. Science is used to
raise money for the expeditions, but
you really climb for the hell of it.**

—Sir Edmund Hillary, New Zealand Mountaineer

**I cannot endure to waste anything
so precious as autumnal sunshine
by staying in the house.**

—NATHANIEL HAWTHORNE, *THE AMERICAN NOTEBOOKS*

Nature abhors a vacuum, and if
I can only walk with sufficient
carelessness I am sure to be filled.

—HENRY DAVID THOREAU

The most beautiful gift of nature is that
it gives one pleasure to look around
and try to comprehend what we see.

—ALBERT EINSTEIN

Hunting, fishing, drawing, and music
occupied my every moment. Cares I knew
not, and cared naught about them.

—JOHN JAMES AUDUBON

For me, a holiday is about taking a book and going to a mountain and reading.

—Sonam Kapoor, Indian Actor

Every good hike brings you eventually back home. Right where you started.

—Edward Abbey, *The Journey Home*

The sun does not shine for a few trees and flowers, but for the wide world's joy.

—Henry Ward Beecher

I hope I have found myself, my work, my happiness, under the light of the Western skies.

—Zane Grey

I think that the only thing that can
bring us into a place of fullness is
being out in the land with other.

—TERRY TEMPEST WILLIAMS, *A VOICE IN THE WILDERNESS:
CONVERSATIONS WITH TERRY TEMPEST WILLIAMS*

The best climber is the one
who has the most fun.

—ALEX LOWE, AMERICAN CLIMBER

I never saw a discontented tree.

—JOHN MUIR

It has always been a happy thought
to me that the creek runs on all
night, new every minute.

— ANNIE DILLARD, *PILGRIM AT TINKER CREEK*

I was happy in the midst of
dangers and inconveniences.

—Daniel Boone

**Poking at a campfire with a stick is
one of life's great satisfactions.**

—Patrick F. McManus, Humor Writer

In wilderness one experiences
exhilaration and joy.

—Harvey Broome, *Out Under Sky Of Great Smokies:
A Personal Journal*

When I rise up let me rise up joyful
like a bird. When I fall let me fall
without regret like a leaf.

—Wendell Berry

I gave my heart to the mountains the
minute I stood beside this river . . .

—WALLACE STEGNER, *WALLACE STEGNER AND THE*
CONTINENTAL VISION: ESSAYS ON LITERATURE,
HISTORY, AND LANDSCAPE

In the woods too, a man casts off his
years, as the snake his slough, and at
what period soever of life, is always a
child. In the woods, is perpetual youth.

—RALPH WALDO EMERSON, *NATURE AND SELECTED ESSAYS*

**On my afternoon walk I would fain
forget all my morning occupations
and my obligations to society.**

—HENRY DAVID THOREAU

I don't like either the word [hike] or
the thing. People ought to saunter
in the mountains—not "hike!"

—JOHN MUIR

**A journey into the wilderness is the
freest, cheapest, most nonprivileged
of pleasures. Anyone with two legs
and the price of a pair of army
surplus combat boots may enter.**

—EDWARD ABBEY

A walk in nature walks the soul back home.

—MARY DAVIS, AUTHOR

We both loved the birds and animals and plants. We both felt far happier out of doors.

—TRACY REES, *AMY SNOW*

Fishing is a condition of the mind wherein one cannot have a bad time.

—ZANE GREY

He is richest who is content with the least, for content is the wealth of nature.

—SOCRATES

There is a pleasure in the pathless woods,
There is a rapture on the lonely shore,
There is society, where none intrudes,
By the deep Sea, and music in its roar:
I love not Man the less, but Nature more...

—LORD BYRON, "CHILDE HAROLD'S PILGRIMAGE"

I love to sit on a mountain top and gaze. I don't think of anything but the people I care about and the view.

—JULIAN LENNON

I fancied my luck to be witnessing yet another full moon.

—ROMAN PAYNE, NOVELIST & POET

I am extremely happy walking on the downs . . . I like to have space to spread my mind out in.

—VIRGINIA WOOLF, DIARY EXCERPT

HEALING

I go to nature to be soothed and healed, and to
have my senses put in order.

—JOHN BURROUGHS

Those who dwell among the beauties
and mysteries of the earth are
never alone or weary of life.

—RACHEL CARSON, *THE SENSE OF WONDER*

**Smart people that like good health
spend several hours outdoors
daily in the shade of trees.**

—STEVEN MAGEE, *SOLAR RADIATION, GLOBAL
WARMING AND HUMAN DISEASE*

My father considered a walk among the
mountains as the equivalent of churchgoing.

—ALDOUS HUXLEY

You are one with your skis and nature. This is something that develops not only the body but the soul as well, and it has a deeper meaning for a people than most of us perceive.

—Fridtjof Nansen, Norwegian Explorer

"The wilderness once offered men a plausible way of life," the doctor said. "Now it functions as a psychiatric refuge."

—Edward Abbey, *The Monkey Wrench Gang*

Keep close to Nature's heart . . . and break clear away, once in a while, and climb a mountain or spend a week in the woods. Wash your spirit clean.

—John Muir

I didn't go up there to die. I
went up there to live.

—REINHOLD MESSNER, ITALIAN MOUNTAINEER

My spiritual life is found inside
the heart of the wild.

—TERRY TEMPEST WILLIAMS, *THE HOUR OF LAND: A
PERSONAL TOPOGRAPHY OF AMERICA'S NATIONAL PARKS*

**I believe that there is a subtle magnetism
in Nature, which, if we unconsciously
yield to it, will direct us aright.**

—HENRY DAVID THOREAU

Mountains have long been a geography
for pilgrimage, place where people have
been humbled and strengthened, they
are symbols of the sacred center.

—JOAN HALIFAX, *THE FRUITFUL DARKNESS: A JOURNEY
THROUGH BUDDHIST PRACTICE AND TRIBAL WISDOM*

As we work to heal the earth,
the earth heals us.

—ROBIN WALL KIMMERER, *BRAIDING SWEETGRASS: INDIGENOUS WISDOM, SCIENTIFIC KNOWLEDGE, AND THE TEACHINGS OF PLANTS*

As the fisherman depends upon the rivers, lakes and seas, and the farmer upon the land for his existence, so does mankind in general depend upon the beauty of the world about him for his spiritual and emotional existence.

—ANSEL ADAMS, *ANSEL ADAMS: OUR NATIONAL PARKS,* FROM A SPEECH TO THE WILDERNESS SOCIETY, MAY 9, 1980

Come to the woods for here is rest.

—JOHN MUIR

In the woods, we return to reason and faith.

—RALPH WALDO EMERSON

There was a freshness and breeziness, too, and an exhilarating sense of emancipation from all sorts of cares and responsibilities, that almost made us feel that the years we had spent in the close, hot city, toiling and slaving, had been wasted and thrown away.

—MARK TWAIN, *ROUGHING IT*

Mountains are not stadiums where I satisfy my ambition to achieve, they are the cathedrals where I practice my religion.

—ANATOLI BOUKREEV, RUSSIAN MOUNTAINEER

It's amazing the difference
a bit of sky can make.

—SHEL SILVERSTEIN, *WHERE THE SIDEWALK ENDS*

Society, as we have constituted it, will have no place for me, has none to offer; but Nature, whose sweet rains fall on unjust and just alike, will have clefts in the rocks where I may hide, and secret valleys in whose silence I may weep undisturbed. She will hang the night with stars so that I may walk abroad in the darkness without stumbling, and send the wind over my footprints so that none may track me to my hurt: she will cleanse me in great waters, and with bitter herbs make me whole.

—OSCAR WILDE, *DE PROFUNDIS*

Every step of the walk unburdens us
of what we have just seen and thought
while it simultaneously thrusts us
into the previously unknown.

—Jeffrey Robinson, Author

**The best remedy for those who are afraid,
lonely or unhappy is to go outside.**

—Anne Frank

In God's wildness lies the hope of the
world—the great fresh unblighted,
unredeemed wilderness. The galling
harness of civilization drops off, and
wounds heal ere we are aware.

—John Muir

To live only for some future goal is shallow. It's the sides of the mountain that sustain life, not the top.

—ROBERT M. PIRSIG, *ZEN AND THE ART OF MOTORCYCLE MAINTENANCE: AN INQUIRY INTO VALUES*

Let every step you take upon the earth be as a prayer.

—BLACK ELK

Some old fashioned things, like fresh air and sunshine are hard to beat.

—LAURA INGALLS WILDER

There is something infinitely healing in the repeated refrains of nature— the assurance that dawn comes after night, and spring after winter.

—RACHEL CARSON, *THE SENSE OF WONDER*

Mountains seem to answer an increasing imaginative need in the West. More and more people are discovering a desire for them, and a powerful solace in them.

—ROBERT MACFARLANE, *MOUNTAINS OF THE MIND: ADVENTURES IN REACHING THE SUMMIT*

Earth has no sorrow that earth can not heal.

—JOHN MUIR

We need the tonic of wildness . . . At the same time that we are earnest to explore and learn all things, we require that all things be mysterious and unexplorable, that land and sea be indefinitely wild, unsurveyed and unfathomed by us because unfathomable. We can never have enough of nature.

—HENRY DAVID THOREAU, *WALDEN*

. . . as harsh as the empty lands were,
they possessed a grace and a beauty
that no artifice could compete with
and that he found restorative.

—CHRISTOPHER PAOLINI, *INHERITANCE*

I have two doctors, my left leg and my right.

—G. M. TREVELYAN, BRITISH HISTORIAN

We don't stop hiking because we grow old,
we grow old because we stop hiking.

—FINIS MITCHELL, AMERICAN MOUNTAINEER

**One day I undertook a tour through
the country, and the diversity and
beauties of nature I met with in this
charming season, expelled every
gloomy and vexatious thought.**

—DANIEL BOONE

**Walking: the most ancient exercise
and still the best modern exercise.**

—Carrie Latet, Screenwriter

Chasing angels or fleeing demons,
go to the mountains.

—Jeffrey Rasley, *Bringing Progress to Paradise: What
I Got from Giving to a Mountain Village in Nepal*

We go to Nature for comfort in trouble,
and sympathy in joy, only in books.
Admiration of those beauties of the
inanimate world, which modern poetry
so largely and so eloquently describes,
is not, even in the best of us, one of
the original instincts of our nature.

—Wilkie Collins, *The Woman in White*

Wilderness to the people of America is a spiritual necessity, an antidote to the high pressure of modern life, a means of regaining serenity and equilibrium.

—SIGURD F. OLSON, "WE NEED WILDERNESS," *NATIONAL PARKS MAGAZINE*, JANUARY–MARCH 1946

Rest is not idleness, and to lie sometimes on the grass under trees on a summer's day, listening to the murmur of the water, or watching the clouds float across the sky, is by no means a waste of time.

—JOHN LUBBOCK, *THE USE OF LIFE*

Spiritual renewal occurs in the wilderness.

—LAILAH GIFTY AKITA, GHANAIAN AND FOUNDER OF SMART YOUTH VOLUNTEERS FOUNDATION

Climb the mountains and get their good tidings. Nature's peace will flow into you as sunshine flows into trees. The winds will blow their own freshness into you, and the storms their energy, while cares will drop off like autumn leaves.

—JOHN MUIR

Walking is a man's best medicine.

—HIPPOCRATES

There is something in the very name of wilderness, which charms the ear, and soothes the spirit of man.

—ESTWICK EVANS, *EARLY WESTERN TRAVELS*

To forget how to dig the earth and to tend the soil is to forget ourselves.

—MAHATMA GANDHI

I go to books and to nature as the
bee goes to a flower, for a nectar that
I can make into my own honey.

—John Burroughs

I think that I cannot preserve my health
and spirits, unless I spend four hours a
day at least—and it is commonly more
than that—sauntering through the woods
and over the hills and fields, absolutely
free from all worldly engagements.

—Henry David Thoreau

**Nature, time and patience are
the three great physicians.**

—Chinese Proverb

Keep calm. You have the forest in your blood.

—Nenia Campbell, *Black Beast*

Be healthy by being outdoors in the natural daylight with nature!

—Steven Magee, *Light Forensics*

We are now in the mountains and they are in us, kindling enthusiasm, making every nerve quiver, filling every pore and cell of us.

—John Muir

I am permanently affected by those solitary encounters with land, sky, and water, and all that's contained within.

—Jeff Rasley, Adventure Writer

There are moments when all anxiety and stated toil are becalmed in the infinite leisure and repose of nature.

—Henry David Thoreau

It is not so much for its beauty that
the forest makes a claim upon men's
hearts, as for that subtle something,
that quality of air that emanation
from old trees, that so wonderfully
changes and renews a weary spirit.

—ROBERT LOUIS STEVENSON

**Let the sounds of nature amplify
your vibrations of peace.**

—PATRICK ZEIS, MEDITATION INSTRUCTOR

. . . there is something which impresses the
mind with awe in the shade and silence
of these vast forests. In the deep solitude,
alone with nature, we converse with God.

—THADDEUS MASON HARRIS, HARVARD
LIBRARIAN & AUTHOR

You can never conquer the mountain.

You can only conquer yourself.

—Jim Whittaker, American Mountaineer

Everybody needs beauty as well as bread,
places to play in and pray in, where nature
may heal and give strength to body and soul.

—John Muir

I go to nature every day for

inspiration in the day's work.

—Frank Lloyd Wright

I felt a peace in nature that I could
never find in the human world.

—Tracy Rees, *Amy Snow*

LESSONS

Nature becomes your teacher, and from her
you will learn what is beautiful and who you
are and what is your special quest in life
and whither you should go . . .

—STEPHEN GRAHAM, *THE ART OF TRAMPING*

Wilderness gave us knowledge.

Wilderness made us human.

—BOYD NORTON, *SERENGETI: THE ETERNAL BEGINNING*

If nature has taught us anything it is
that the impossible is probable.

—ILYAS KASSAM, AUTHOR

We often forget that WE ARE NATURE.
Nature is not something separate
from us. So when we say that we have
lost our connection to nature, we've
lost our connection to ourselves.

—ANDY GOLDSWORTHY, BRITISH SCULPTOR,
PHOTOGRAPHER, & ENVIRONMENTALIST

It's very, very dangerous to lose
contact with living nature.

—ALBERT HOFMANN, SWISS SCIENTIST

In every walk with nature, one
received far more than he seeks.

—JOHN MUIR

Somewhere between the bottom of the
climb and the summit is the answer
to the mystery why we climb.

—GREG CHILD, AUSTRALIAN MOUNTAINEER

Every falling leaf reminds me that I too
will soon be separated from these trees.

—DANIEL J. RICE, *THIS SIDE OF A WILDERNESS*

**I pray to the birds because they remind
me of what I love rather than what
I fear. And at the end of my prayers,
they teach me how to listen.**

—TERRY TEMPEST WILLIAMS, *REFUGE: AN UNNATURAL
HISTORY OF FAMILY AND PLACE*

How to get the best of it all? One must conquer, achieve, get to the top; one must know the end to be convinced that one can win the end—to know there's no dream that musn't be dared. Is this the summit, crowning the day? How cool and quiet! We're not exultant; but delighted, joyful, soberly astonished. Have we vanquished an enemy? None but ourselves. Have we gained success? That word means nothing here. Have we won a kingdom? No and yes. We have achieved an ultimate satisfaction fulfilled a destiny. To struggle and to understand—never this last without the other; such is the law.

—George Leigh Mallory, English Mountaineer

However far or long you plod, you are always in the same place: in the woods.

—BILL BRYSON, *A WALK IN THE WOODS: REDISCOVERING AMERICA ON THE APPALACHIAN TRAIL*

Mountains teach that not everything in this world can be rationally explained.

—ALEKSANDER LWOW, POLISH MOUNTAINEER

Some people when they have taken too much and have been driven beyond the point of endurance, simply crumble and give up. There are others, though they are not many, who will for some reason always be unconquerable. You meet them in time of war and also in time of peace. They have an indomitable spirit and nothing, neither pain nor torture nor threat of death, will cause them to give up.

—ROALD DAHL

If the going is tough and the pressure is on,
If the reserves of strength have been drained
and the summit is still not in sight, then the
quality to seek in the person is neither great
strength nor quickness of hand, but rather
a resolute mind firmly set on its purpose
that refuses to let its body slack or rest.

—Sir Edmund Hillary, New Zealand Mountaineer

**Scholars, I plead with you, Where are your
dictionaries of the wind, the grasses?**

—Norman MacCaig, Scottish Poet

We still do not know one thousandth of one
percent of what nature has revealed to us.

—Albert Einstein

Nature has been for me, for as long as I remember, a source of solace, inspiration, adventure, and delight; a home, a teacher, a companion.

—LORRAINE ANDERSON, AMERICAN NATURE WRITER

The happiest man is he who learns from nature the lesson of worship.

—RALPH WALDO EMERSON

They are able who think they are able.

—VIRGIL

When you're in the wild, there's nothing to hide behind.

—SHANNON M MULLEN, *SEE WHAT FLOWERS*

It's strange how deserts turn us into believers. I believe in walking in a landscape of mirages, because you learn humility. I believe in living in a land of little water because life is drawn together. And I believe in the gathering of bones as a testament to spirits that have moved on. If the desert is holy, it is because it is a forgotten place that allows us to remember the sacred. Perhaps that is why every pilgrimage to the desert is a pilgrimage to the self.

—Terry Tempest Williams, *Red: Passion and Patience in the Desert*

Jumping from boulder to boulder and
never falling, with a heavy pack, is easier
than it sounds; you just can't fall when
you get into the rhythm of the dance.

—Jack Kerouac, *The Dharma Bums*

It thus emerges that, for young people and
adults alike, Outdoor Adventure is perceived
as a vehicle for building values and ideals,
for developing creativity and enterprise, for
enhancing a sense of citizenship, and for
widening physical and spiritual horizons.

—Lord Hunt of Llanfair Waterdine

There's only one way to gain mountain sense,
and that's to be in the mountains a lot.

—Alex Lowe, American Climber

By endurance we conquer.

—Ernest Shackleton, British Explorer

Live in each season as it passes; breathe
the air, drink the drink, taste the fruit, and
resign yourself to the influence of the earth.

—Henry David Thoreau, *Walden*

Those honor nature well, who teach
that she can speak on everything.

—Blaise Pascal, *Pensées*

There is a way that nature speaks,
that land speaks. Most of the time we
are simply not patient enough, quiet
enough to pay attention to the story.

—Linda Hogan, Author

I wondered what those mountains
behind them might tell me, what advice
they would give, if they could talk.

—SHANNON HUFFMAN POLSON, *NORTH OF HOPE: A
DAUGHTER'S ARCTIC JOURNEY*

**It is good to have an end to journey
toward; but it is the journey
that matters, in the end.**

—URSULA K. LE GUIN, *THE LEFT HAND OF DARKNESS*

Each fresh peak ascended teaches something.

—SIR MARTIN CONWAY

Trees and stones will teach you that which
you can never learn from masters.

—ST. BERNARD DE CLAIRVAUX

Up! up! my Friend, and quit your books;
Or surely you'll grow double:
Up! up! my Friend, and clear your looks;
Why all this toil and trouble?

The sun above the mountain's head,
A freshening lustre mellow
Through all the long green fields has spread,
His first sweet evening yellow.

Books! 'tis a dull and endless strife:
Come, hear the woodland linnet,
How sweet his music! on my life,
There's more of wisdom in it.

And hark! how blithe the throstle sings!
He, too, is no mean preacher:
Come forth into the light of things,
Let Nature be your teacher.

She has a world of ready wealth,
Our minds and hearts to bless—
Spontaneous wisdom breathed by health,
Truth breathed by cheerfulness.

One impulse from a vernal wood
May teach you more of man,
Of moral evil and of good,
Than all the sages can.

Sweet is the lore which Nature brings;
Our meddling intellect
Mis-shapes the beauteous forms of things:—
We murder to dissect.

Enough of Science and of Art;
Close up those barren leaves;
Come forth, and bring with you a heart
That watches and receives.

—WILLIAM WORDSWORTH, "THE TABLES TURNED"

. . . the wilderness is alive, that its whispers
are there for all to hear—and to respond to.

—Lawrence Anthony, *The Elephant Whisperer*

**It's the idea that people living close to
nature tend to be noble. It's seeing all
those sunsets that does it. You can't
watch a sunset and then go off and
set fire to your neighbor's tepee.**

—Daniel Quinn, *Ishmael*

To the question: Wilderness, who
needs it? Doc would say: Because we
like the taste of freedom, comrades.

—Edward Abbey, *The Monkey Wrench Gang*

Let us draw a lesson from nature,
which always works by short ways.
When the fruit is ripe, it falls.

—RALPH WALDO EMERSON

You need mountains, long staircases
don't make good hikers.

—AMIT KALANTRI, *WEALTH OF WORDS*

Wilderness is a form of sophistication,
because it carries within it true
knowledge of our place in the world.

—MARTIN SHAW, ENGLISH ACTOR

The sea, the great unifier, is man's only hope.
Now, as never before, the old phrase has a
literal meaning: we are all in the same boat.

—JACQUES YVES COUSTEAU, FRENCH EXPLORER

Wilderness, or wildness is a mystique. A religion, an intense philosophy, a dream of ideal society—these are also mystique.

—ANSEL ADAMS, *ANSEL ADAMS*, FROM A SPEECH TO THE WILDERNESS SOCIETY, MAY 9, 1980

Strong motivation is the most important factor in getting you to the top.

—SIR EDMUND HILLARY, NEW ZEALAND MOUNTAINEER

Everyone has their own Everest to climb.

—WANDA RUTKIEWICZ, POLISH MOUNTAINEER

It is the marriage of the soul with nature that makes the intellect fruitful, and gives birth to imagination.

—HENRY DAVID THOREAU

As long as you believe what you're doing
is meaningful, you can cut through fear
and exhaustion and take the next step.

—ARLENE BLUM, AMERICAN MOUNTAINEER

**It is better to go skiing and think of God,
than go to church and think of sport.**

—FRIDTJOF NANSEN, NORWEGIAN EXPLORER

Much of human behavior can be explained
by watching the wild beasts around us.

—SUZY KASSEM, *RISE UP AND SALUTE THE SUN:
THE WRITINGS OF SUZY KASSEM*

When you are lost in the wilderness, a tree
will always point you in the right direction.

—ANTHONY T. HINCKS, AUTHOR

**Every mountain top is within reach
if you just keep climbing.**

—BARRY FINLAY, *KILIMANJARO AND BEYOND*

It has always been my understanding
that truth and freedom can
only exist in wild places.

— DANIEL J. RICE, *THE UNPEOPLED SEASON: JOURNAL
FROM A NORTH COUNTRY WILDERNESS*

**Nature is indifferent to our
love, but never unfaithful.**

—EDWARD ABBEY

Nature puts no question and answers
none which we mortals ask. She has
long ago taken her resolution.

—HENRY DAVID THOREAU

If you will stay close to nature, to its simplicity, to the small things hardly noticeable, those things can unexpectedly become great and immeasurable.

—RAINER MARIA RILKE, *LETTERS TO A YOUNG POET*

Nature is just enough; but men and women must comprehend and accept her suggestions.

—ANTOINETTE BROWN BLACKWELL, FIRST FEMALE ORDAINED PROTESTANT MINISTER IN THE US

Love is life's snow. It falls deepest and softest into the gashes left by the fight— whiter and purer than snow itself.

—FRIDTJOF NANSEN, NORWEGIAN EXPLORER

. . . we disconnect ourselves from
nature and the wilderness too many
times. Our birthplace. Our home.

—JELLIS VAES, ADVENTURER

The mountains have rules. they are
harsh rules, but they are there, and
if you keep to them you are safe.

—WALTER BONATTI, ITALIAN MOUNTAINEER

Knowing trees, I understand the
meaning of patience. Knowing grass,
I can appreciate persistence.

—ROBERT FROST

Adopt the pace of nature:
her secret is patience.

—RALPH WALDO EMERSON

It is self-evident that nothing educates an eye for the features of a landscape so well as the practice of measuring it by your own legs.

—Sir Leslie Stephen, English Author

Life in the wild, as I'm observing, is about survival as much as pleasure.

—Fennel Hudson, *A Waterside Year—Fennel's Journal—No. 2*

One should pay attention to even the smallest crawling creature for these too may have a valuable lesson to teach us.

—Black Elk

It is a commonplace of all religious thought, even the most primitive, that the man seeking visions and insight must go apart from his fellows and live for a time in the wilderness.

—LOREN EISELEY, AMERICAN PHILOSOPHER

It's always further than it looks. It's always taller than it looks. And it's always harder than it looks.

—REINHOLD MESSNER, ITALIAN MOUNTAINEER

That's the purity of nature. It may be harsh in its honesty, but it never lies to you. . .

—CARINE MCCANDLESS, *THE WILD TRUTH: A MEMOIR*

Sit down before fact as a little child, be
prepared to give up every preconceived
notion, follow humbly wherever and
to whatever abysses nature leads,
or you shall learn nothing.

—THOMAS HENRY HUXLEY, ENGLISH BIOLOGIST

Don't judge each day by the harvest
you reap but by the seeds you plant.

—ROBERT LOUIS STEVENSON

The first in time and the first in importance
of the influences upon the mind is
that of nature. Every day, the sun; and,
after sunset, night and her stars.

—RALPH WALDO EMERSON

Like music and art, love of nature is a common language that can transcend political or social boundaries.

—JIMMY CARTER

The wilderness holds answers to questions man has not yet learned to ask.

—NANCY NEWHALL, AMERICAN PHOTOGRAPHY CRITIC

Carry as little as possible, but choose that little with care.

—EARL SHAFFER, FIRST PERSON TO WALK THE ENTIRE APPALACHIAN TRAIL

It's mostly during times of wilderness experience, that people are willing to accept the lessons that wisdom teaches.

—SUNDAY ADELAJA, PASTOR

There are in nature neither rewards nor
punishments—there are consequences.

—Robert G. Ingersoll, American Lawyer

When one tugs at a single thing in nature,
he finds it attached to the rest of the world.

—John Muir

The world of nature, at once a vision
of exquisite beauty and an arena
of brutal savagery, is a dynamic
system of delicate balances.

—S. Bradley Stoner, *Prey for Survival*

**Study nature, love nature, stay close
to nature. It will never fail you.**

—Frank Lloyd Wright

**In the spring, at the end of the day,
you should smell like dirt.**

—MARGARET ATWOOD, *BLUEBEARD'S EGG*

Generally speaking, a howling wilderness
does not howl: it is the imagination of
the traveler that does the howling.

—HENRY DAVID THOREAU

**It seems to me that we all look at Nature
too much, and live with her too little.**

—OSCAR WILDE, *DE PROFUNDIS*

Among wilderness survival tips,
punching a wild animal in the face
probably isn't on a checklist.

—Kat Kruger, *The Night Has Teeth*

You never climb the same mountain twice,
not even in memory. Memory rebuilds
the mountain, changes the weather,
retells the jokes, remakes all the moves.

—Lito Tejada-Flores, Author

REFLECTION

The real voyage of discovery consists not in
seeking new landscapes, but in having new eyes.

—MARCEL PROUST

Perhaps the Wilderness we fear is the pause between our own heartbeats, the silence that reminds us we live by grace.

—TERRY TEMPEST WILLIAMS, *RED: PASSION AND PATIENCE IN THE DESERT*

Look into nature, and then you will understand it better.

—ALBERT EINSTEIN

Gaze not too long into the abyss, lest the abyss gaze into thee.

—EDWARD ABBEY, *DESERT SOLITAIRE*

I look back on tremendous efforts and exhaustion and dismal looking out of a tent door on to a dismal world of snow and vanishing hopes—and yet, and yet, and yet there have been a good many things to see the other side.

—GEORGE LEIGH MALLORY, ENGLISH MOUNTAINEER,
DIARY ENTRY (MAY 27, 1924)

Climbing is a great effort, but
the extraordinary pleasure.

—JERZY KUKUCZKA, POLISH CLIMBER

I only went out for a walk, and finally
concluded to stay out till sundown, for
going out, I found, was really going in.

—JOHN MUIR

A great many people, and more all the
time, live their entire lives without ever
once sleeping out under the stars.

—ALAN S. KESSELHEIM, *LET THEM PADDLE:
COMING OF AGE ON THE WATER*

Nature will bear the closest inspection.
She invites us to lay our eye level
with her smallest leaf, and take
an insect view of its plain.

—HENRY DAVID THOREAU

**"I like the mountains because they make
me feel small," Jeff says. "They help me
sort out what's important in life."**

—MARK OBMASCIK, *HALFWAY TO HEAVEN:
MY WHITE-KNUCKLED—AND KNUCKLEHEADED—QUEST
FOR THE ROCKY MOUNTAIN HIGH*

A human being is a part of the whole called by us universe, a part limited in time and space. He experiences himself, his thoughts and feeling as something separated from the rest, a kind of optical delusion of his consciousness. This delusion is a kind of prison for us, restricting us to our personal desires and to affection for a few persons nearest to us. Our task must be to free ourselves from this prison by widening our circle of compassion to embrace all living creatures and the whole of nature in its beauty.

—Albert Einstein

Walking makes the world much
bigger and thus more interesting. You
have time to observe the details.

—Edward Abbey

. . . in order to be found we must
go into the wilderness. Sometimes,
it is only in the getting lost that we
can find our way back home.

—Jeanette LeBlanc, *Wild Heart Writing: A 30-Day
Course to Rediscover Your Deepest Truths*

Normality is a paved road; it's comfortable
to walk, but no flowers grow.

—Vincent van Gogh

You can feel the anarchy and wilderness through words, and the peace and heavens as well.

—Yash Thakur, Indian Cricketer

There's no dream too big for the wilderness.

—Alice Valdal, *Her One and Only*

There is a patience of the wild—dogged, tireless, persistent as life itself—that holds motionless for endless hours the spider in its web, the snake in its coils, the panther in its ambuscade; this patience belongs peculiarly to life when it hunts its living food.

—Jack London, *Call of the Wild*

You look around and lose yourself
in the mountains, rivers, forests or
tundra, but you can see nothing except
for the chaos in your own mind.

—SHANNON M. MULLEN, *SEE WHAT FLOWERS*

To those devoid of imagination a blank
place on the map is a useless waste;
to others, the most valuable part.

—ALDO LEOPOLD, *A SAND COUNTY ALMANAC*
AND SKETCHES HERE AND THERE

Do not harbour any bitterness, it will
lead you straight into the wilderness.

—GIFT GUGU MONA, POET

An increasing number of people who lead
mental lives of great intensity, people
who are sensitive by nature, notice the
steadily more frequent appearance in
them of mental states of great strangeness
. . . a wordless and irrational feeling
of ecstasy; or a breath of psychic pain;
a sense of being spoken to from afar,
from the sky or the sea; an agonizingly
developed sense of hearing which can
cause one to wince at the murmuring
of unseen atoms; an irrational staring
into the heart of some closed kingdom
suddenly and briefly revealed.

—KNUT HAMSUN, AWARDED THE NOBEL PRIZE
IN LITERATURE IN 1920

If we allow ourselves contemplative
time in nature . . . then we can hear
the voice of our conscience.

—Terry Tempest Williams

Deep down, at the molecular heart of life,
the trees and we are essentially identical.

—Carl Sagan, American Astronomer

**The longer I climb, the less important
the goal seems to me, the more
indifferent I become to myself.**

—Reinhold Messner, Italian Mountaineer

Perhaps the truth depends on
a walk around the lake.

—Wallace Stevens, "Notes Toward a Supreme Fiction"

I find that in contemplating the natural
world my pleasure is greater if there
are not too many others contemplating
it with me, at the same time.

—Edward Abbey, *Desert Solitaire*

**Returning home is the most difficult
part of long-distance hiking; You
have grown outside the puzzle
and your piece no longer fits.**

—Cindy Ross, *Journey on the Quest*

Let our souls be mountains, Let our spirits
be stars, Let our hearts be worlds.

—Ansel Adams

I felt like lying down by the side of the trail and remembering it all. The woods do that to you, they always look familiar, long lost, like the face of a long-dead relative, like an old dream, like a piece of forgotten song drifting across the water, most of all like golden eternities of past childhood or past manhood and all the living and the dying and the heartbreak that went on a million years ago and the clouds as they pass overhead seem to testify (by their own lonesome familiarity) to this feeling.

—JACK KEROUAC, *THE DHARMA BUMS*

The lover of nature is he whose inward
and outward senses are still truly adjusted
to each other; who has retained the spirit
of infancy even into the era of manhood.
His intercourse with heaven and earth,
becomes part of his daily food.

—RALPH WALDO EMERSON

We are not apart from nature but a part of it.

—TERRY TEMPEST WILLIAMS

**It's not the Mountain we
conquer, but ourselves.**

—SIR EDMUND HILLARY, NEW ZEALAND MOUNTAINEER

. . . there's a silent voice in the wilderness that
we hear only when no one else is around.

—ROB SCHULTHEIS, *FOOL'S GOLD: LIVES, LOVES, AND
MISADVENTURES IN THE FOUR CORNERS COUNTRY*

I come into the peace of wild things who do not tax their lives with forethought of grief.

—Wendell Berry, "Poem: The Peace of Wild Things"

The goal of life is to make your heartbeat match the beat of the universe, to match your nature with Nature.

—Joseph Campbell, American Author

For I have learned to look on nature, not as in the hour of thoughtless youth; but hearing oftentimes the still, sad music of humanity.

—William Wordsworth, "Lines Composed a Few Miles above Tintern Abbey" (1798)

Climbing is not a battle with the elements, nor against the law of gravity. It's a battle against oneself.

—Walter Bonatti, Italian Mountaineer

I follow the lines of my body on the stone in front of me, spreading my arms as wings, and bathe in the beauty of existence.

—DEAN POTTER, AMERICAN CLIMBER

The stars were shining, and the leaves rustled in the woods ever so mournful; and I heard an owl, away off, who-whooing about somebody that was dead, and a whippowill and a dog crying about somebody that was going to die; and the wind was trying to whisper something to me, and I couldn't make out what it was, and so it made the cold shivers run over me.

—MARK TWAIN, *THE ADVENTURES OF HUCKLEBERRY FINN*

True solitude is found in the wild
places, where one is without human
obligation. One's inner voices become
audible . . . In consequence, one
responds more clearly to other lives.

—Wendell Berry

Ordinarily, I go to the woods alone, with
not a single friend, for they are all smilers
and talkers and therefore unsuitable.

—Mary Oliver

The quality of place, the reaction to
immediate contact with earth and growing
things that have a fugal relationship with
mountains and sky, is essential to the
integrity of our existence on this planet.

—Ansel Adams

O Solitude! if I must with thee dwell,

Let it not be among the jumbled heap

Of murky buildings; climb with me the steep,—

Nature's observatory—whence the dell,

Its flowery slopes, its river's crystal swell,

May seem a span; let me thy vigils keep

'Mongst boughs pavillion'd,

where the deer's swift leap

Startles the wild bee from the fox-glove bell.

But though I'll gladly trace

these scenes with thee,

Yet the sweet converse of an innocent mind,

Whose words are images of thoughts refin'd,

Is my soul's pleasure; and it sure must be

Almost the highest bliss of human-kind,

When to thy haunts two kindred spirits flee.

—John Keats, "Sonnet VII [O Solitude!]"

. . . a conversation of sorts has been
unfolding in this lonesome hollow.
It is not a language like Russian or
Chinese but it is a language nonetheless,
and it is older than the forest.

—JOHN VAILLANT, *THE TIGER: A TRUE STORY
OF VENGEANCE AND SURVIVAL*

If you reconnect with nature and the
wilderness you will not only find the
meaning of life, but you will experience
what it means to be truly alive.

—SYLVIA DOLSON, *JOY OF BEARS*

**The sun illuminates only the eye
of the man, but shines into the
eye and the heart of the child.**

—RALPH WALDO EMERSON

You are nothing but wilderness.

No constraint. No mind.

—TONI MORRISON, *A MERCY*

**The question is not what you
look at, but what you see.**

—HENRY DAVID THOREAU

With what it was like to walk for miles
for no reason other than to witness the
accumulation of trees and meadows,
mountains and deserts, streams and rocks,
rivers and grasses, sunrises and sunsets.

—CHERYL STRAYED, *WILD: FROM LOST TO FOUND
ON THE PACIFIC CREST TRAIL*

**Be alone with your thoughts
and be lost in a wilderness.**

—Anthony T. Hincks, Author

Nature is not only all that is visible
to the eye . . . it also includes the
inner pictures of the soul.

—Edvard Munch, Norwegian Painter

Everything in nature invites us
constantly to be what we are.

—Gretel Ehrlich, American Travel Writer

Wilderness is the capacity to go into
joy, sorrow, and anger fully and stay
there for as long as needed.

—Martin Shaw, English Actor

And into the forest I go, To lose
my mind and find my soul.

—JOHN MUIR

**One climbs, one sees. One descends,
one sees no longer, but one has seen.**

—RENÉ DAUMAL, FRENCH WRITER

The wilderness is a place that every
believer has to experience to be
molded for their divine purpose.

—E'YEN A. GARDNER, *HUMBLY SUBMITTING TO CHANGE—
THE WILDERNESS EXPERIENCE*

I've loved the stars too fondly
to be fearful of the night.

—GALILEO GALILEI

Light up a campfire, and everyone's a storyteller.

—JOHN GEDDES, AMERICAN JOURNALIST

For all the toll the desert takes of a man it gives compensations, deep breaths, deep sleep, and the communion of the stars.

—MARY HUNTER AUSTIN, AMERICAN WRITER

Now I see the secret of making the best person, it is to grow in the open air and to eat and sleep with the earth.

—WALT WHITMAN

Wilderness is not only a condition of nature, but a state of mind and mood and heart.

—ANSEL ADAMS

A man does not climb a mountain without bringing some of it away with him, and leaving something of himself upon it.

—SIR MARTIN CONWAY

Nature does not hurry, yet everything is accomplished.

—LAO TZU

The least movement is of importance to all nature. The entire ocean is affected by a pebble.

—BLAISE PASCAL

To the eyes of the man of imagination, nature is imagination itself.

—WILLIAM BLAKE

Nature is loved by what is best in us.

—Ralph Waldo Emerson

He stood there a moment, listened
to the creek, and let the mountain
air blow against his face.

— Eowyn Ivey, *The Snow Child*

He loved the woods, where it seemed to him
that every life was secret, including his own.

—Wendell Berry

**I sit and listen to the music of water
dripping on a distant stone.**

—John A. Haines, *The Owl in the Mask of the
Dreamer: Collected Poems*

Autumn is the mellower season, and what we
lose in flowers we more than gain in fruits.

—Samuel Butler

**Every man should pull a boat over
a mountain once in his life.**

—Werner Herzog

A flutter of snow, a shower of rain, This
day will not come around again.

—Rose Milligan, "Dust If You Must"

The farther one gets into the wilderness, the greater is the attraction of its lonely freedom.

—THEODORE ROOSEVELT

The best journeys in life are those that answer questions you never thought to ask.

—RICK RIDGEWAY

The color of springtime is in the flowers; the color of winter is in the imagination.

—TERRI GUILLEMETS, AMERICAN WRITER

WHIMSY

All nature wears one universal grin.

—Henry Fielding

Nature rarely surrenders one of
her magnificent secrets.

—ALBERT EINSTEIN

**She wondered if she was the only
person trying not to imagine what
death-by-bear looked like.**

—JAKE VANDER-ARK, *FALLOUT DREAMS*

Trees are the Earth's endless effort
to speak to the listening heaven.

—RABINDRANATH TAGORE, BENGALI POET, MUSICIAN,
AND ARTIST

Maybe kissing is sort of like nature's coffee.

—SCOTT WESTERFELD

I like being near the top of a mountain. One can't get lost here.

—Wisława Szymborska

Good planning is important. I've also regarded a sense of Wit as one of the most important things on a big expedition. When you're in a difficult or dangerous situation, or when you're depressed about the chances of success, someone who can make you laugh eases the tension.

— Sir Edmund Hillary, New Zealand Mountaineer

If you ever, ever, ever meet a grizzly bear, / You must never, never, never ask him where / He is going, / Or what he is doing; / For if you ever, ever dare / To stop a grizzly bear, / You will never meet another grizzly bear.

—Mary Hunter Austin, American Writer

Then came the gadgeteer, otherwise known as the sporting-goods dealer. He has draped the American outdoorsman with an infinity of contraptions, all offered as aids to self-reliance, hardihood, woodcraft, or marksmanship, but too often functioning as substitutes for them. Gadgets fill the pockets, they dangle from neck and belt. The overflow fills the auto-trunk and also the trailer. Each item of outdoor equipment grows lighter and often better, but the aggregate poundage becomes tonnage.

—ALDO LEOPOLD

The stars were better company
anyway. They were very beautiful,
and they almost never snored.

—DAVID EDDINGS, *CRYSTAL GORGE*

**At the first step upon the cold surface,
Buck's feet sank into a white mush
something very like mud. He sprang back
with a snort. More of this white stuff was
falling through the air. He shook himself,
but more of it fell upon him. He sniffed
it curiously, then licked some up on his
tongue. It bit like fire, and the next instant
was gone. This puzzled him. He tried it
again, with the same result. The onlookers
laughed uproariously, and he felt ashamed,
he knew not why, for it was his first snow.**

—JACK LONDON, *CALL OF THE WILD*

Mountain draws ancestors together
in the form of clouds.

—JOAN HALIFAX, THE FRUITFUL DARKNESS: A JOURNEY
THROUGH BUDDHIST PRACTICE AND TRIBAL WISDOM

Some people walk in the rain,
others just get wet.

—ROGER MILLER, SINGER/SONGWRITER

**It's hard for the modern generation
to understand Thoreau, who
lived beside a pond but didn't
own water skis or a snorkel.**

—LOUDON WAINWRIGHT, SINGER/SONGWRITER

It should not be denied . . . that being
footloose has always exhilarated us.

—WALLACE STEGNER, MARKING THE SPARROW'S FALL:
THE MAKING OF THE AMERICAN WEST

Announced by all the trumpets of the sky,

Arrives the snow, and, driving o'er the fields,

Seems nowhere to alight: the whited air

Hides hills and woods, the river, and the heaven,

And veils the farm-house at the garden's end.

The sled and traveller stopped, the courier's feet

Delayed, all friends shut out, the housemates sit

Around the radiant fireplace, enclosed

In a tumultuous privacy of storm.

—

Come see the north wind's masonry.

Out of an unseen quarry evermore

Furnished with tile, the fierce artificer

Curves his white bastions with projected roof

Round every windward stake, or tree, or door.

Speeding, the myriad-handed, his wild work

So fanciful, so savage, nought cares he

For number or proportion. Mockingly,

On coop or kennel he hangs Parian wreaths;

A swan-like form invests the hidden thorn;

Fills up the farmer's lane from wall to wall,

Maugre the farmer's sighs; and, at the gate,

A tapering turret overtops the work.

And when his hours are numbered, and the world

Is all his own, retiring, as he were not,

Leaves, when the sun appears, astonished Art

To mimic in slow structures, stone by stone,

Built in an age, the mad wind's night-work,

The frolic architecture of the snow.

— RALPH WALDO EMERSON, "THE SNOW-STORM"

Wild beach is my primordial address.

—TALISMANIST GIEBRA, TALISMANIST: FRAGMENTS
OF THE ANCIENT FIRE

**There are always bigger fish
than you have caught . . .**

—ZANE GREY

In the spring, I have counted 136 different kinds of weather inside of 24 hours.

—MARK TWAIN

Time is but the stream I go a-fishing in.

—HENRY DAVID THOREAU

After a day's walk, everything
has twice its usual value.

—G. M. TREVELYAN, BRITISH HISTORIAN

I should like the fields tinged with red,
the rivers yellow and the trees painted
blue. Nature has no imagination.

—CHARLES BAUDELAIRE, FRENCH POET

A mountain is not like men.

A mountain is sincere.

—WALTER BONATTI, ITALIAN MOUNTAINEER

It's in the wilderness that rainbows roam free.

—ANTHONY T. HINCKS, AUTHOR

I believe in God, only I spell it Nature.

—FRANK LLOYD WRIGHT

A flower is an educated weed.

—LUTHER BURBANK, AMERICAN BOTANIST

There's a fine line between fishing and
just standing on the shore like an idiot.

—STEVEN WRIGHT, COMEDIAN

One touch of nature makes the whole world kin.

—WILLIAM SHAKESPEARE, *TROILUS AND CRESSIDA*

We love the land. It is a primal affair.

—TERRY TEMPEST WILLIAMS, *AN UNSPOKEN HUNGER*

People from a planet without flowers would think we must be mad with joy the whole time to have such things about us.

—IRIS MURDOCH, *A FAIRLY HONOURABLE DEFEAT*

Any moment, it seemed, the woodland gods, who are to be worshipped in silence and loneliness, might stretch their mighty and terrific outlines among the trees.

—ALGERNON BLACKWOOD, *THE WENDIGO*

If your knees aren't green by
the end of the day, you ought to
seriously re-examine your life.

— BILL WATTERSON, *CALVIN & HOBBES*

I like it when a flower or a little
tuft of grass grows through a crack
in the concrete. It's so heroic.

—GEORGE CARLIN, COMEDIAN

Man is a great blunderer going about
in the woods, and there is no other
except the bear makes so much noise.

—MARY HUNTER AUSTIN

**Go there. Be there. Walk gently
and quietly deep within it.**

—EDWARD ABBEY, *BEYOND THE WALL:
ESSAYS FROM THE OUTSIDE*

The outside is the only place we
can truly be inside the world.

—Daniel J. Rice, *This Side of a Wilderness:
A Novel*

When it rains, look for rainbows in the wild.

—Anthony T. Hincks

**We will stomp to the top with
the wind in our teeth.**

—George Leigh Mallory, English Mountaineer

It isn't the mountain ahead that wears you
out; it's the grain of sand in your shoe.

—Robert W. Service, British-Canadian Poet & Writer

Many men go fishing all of their lives
without knowing that it is fish they are after.

—Henry David Thoreau

**There is no such thing as bad
weather, only bad clothes.**

—James Rebanks, *The Shepherd's Life: A People's
History of the Lake District* (2015)

I've spent as much of my life fishing
as decency allowed, and sometimes I
don't let even that get in my way.

—Thomas McGuane

Choose only one master—nature.

—Rembrandt

The cloud is free only to go with the
wind. The rain is free only in falling.

—WENDELL BERRY

Men argue. Nature acts.

—VOLTAIRE

Remember, a dead fish can float downstream,
but it takes a live one to swim upstream.

—W. C. FIELDS

The sea is a desert of waves,
A wilderness of water.

—LANGSTON HUGHES, *SELECTED POEMS*

If you don't love animals, you'll
never love the wild.

—ANTHONY T. HINCKS, AUTHOR

Ours was a world of eternal spring,
until the summer came.

—Roman Payne, *Hope and Despair*

I am at two with Nature.

—Woody Allen

Every mile is two in winter.

—George Herbert

**I like this place and could
willingly waste my time in it.**

—William Shakespeare

Once upon a time, when women were birds,
there was the simple understanding that
to sing at dawn, and to sing at dusk, was
to heal the world through joy. The birds
still remember what we have forgotten,
that the world is meant to be celebrated.

—Terry Tempest Williams

**A perfect summer day is when the sun is
shining, the breeze is blowing, the birds
are singing, and the lawn mower is broken.**

—James Dent, American Author and Sportswriter

Walk-walk-WALK upon our
sweet and blessed land!

—Edward Abbey, *Desert Solitaire*

You never conquer a mountain. You stand on the summit a few brief minutes and then the wind blows away your footprints.

—ARLENE BLUM, AMERICAN MOUNTAINEER

Trees're always a relief, after people.

—DAVID MITCHELL, *BLACK SWAN GREEN*

Love the trees until their leaves fall off, then encourage them to try again next year.

—CHAD SUGG, SINGER/SONGWRITER

When you fish for love, bait with your heart, not your brain.

—MARK TWAIN

Last year I went fishing with Salvador
Dali. He was using a dotted line.
He caught every other fish.

—STEVEN WRIGHT, COMEDIAN

You can't be suspicious of a tree, or
accuse a bird or a squirrel of subversion
or challenge the ideology of a violet.

—HAROLD "HAL" BORLAND, AMERICAN AUTHOR

A fellow ought to make sure his
canoe is going to stay right side up
before he asks a girl to step into it.

—B. M. BOWER, *THE LOOKOUT MAN*

**The best thing one can do when
it's raining is to let it rain.**

—HENRY WADSWORTH LONGFELLOW

Fishing is very similar to golf because
in both sports you hold a long skinny
thing in your hand while nothing
happens for days at a time.

—DAVE BARRY, SYNDICATED NEWSPAPER COLUMNIST

**Forget not that the earth delights
to feel your bare feet and winds
long to play with your hair.**

—KAHLI GIBRAN, LEBANESE-AMERICAN WRITER

The trees were friendly, they gave
me rest and shadowed refuge.

—ASPEN MATIS, *GIRL IN THE WOODS: A MEMOIR*

Should humans conquer the
mountain or should they wish for
the mountain to possess them?

— KIRAN DESAI, *THE INHERITANCE OF LOSS*

The word hammockable (describing two trees that are the perfect distance apart between which a hammock can be hung) is not in the dictionary, but it should be.

—Dan Kieran, *The Book of Idle Pleasures*

My tent doesn't look like much but, as an estate agent might say, "It is air-conditioned and has exceptional location."

—Fennel Hudson, *A Waterside Year—Fennel's Journal—No. 2*

I have never been lost, but I will admit to being confused for several weeks.

—Daniel Boone

Every man's a would be sportsman, in the dreams of his intent.

—Reuben Anderson

**Mountains have a way of dealing
with overconfidence.**

—HERMANN BUHL

Nature has no mercy at all. Nature
says, I'm going to snow. If you have
on a bikini and no snowshoes, that's
tough. I am going to snow anyway.

—MAYA ANGELOU

Getting to the top is optional.
Getting down is mandatory.

—ED VIESTURS, AMERICAN MOUNTAINEER

Never does Nature say one thing
and Wisdom another.

—JUVENAL, *THE SIXTEEN SATIRES* (127 AD)

**Spring is nature's way of
saying, "Let's party!"**

—Robin Williams

What did the mountains care about
our plan to climb them, rafting
the waters that divided them?

— Erica Ferencik, *The River at Night*

If fishing is a religion, fly
fishing is high church.

—Tom Brokaw, American Broadcast Journalist

**Look! A trickle of water running
through some dirt! I'd say our
afternoon just got booked solid!**

—Bill Watterson, *Calvin & Hobbes*

The butterfly counts not months but moments, and has time enough.

—Rabindranath Tagore, Bengali Poet, Musician, and Artist

Earth is sad, Moon is shy, Sun is happy but wait a moment, I just forgot to tell you that I am the child of open sky.

—Santosh Kalwar, Author

The summit is just the halfway point.

—Ed Viesturs, American Mountaineer

The woods are lovely, dark and deep, but I have promises to keep, and miles to go before I sleep . . .

—Robert Frost

I love not man the less, but Nature more.

—Lord Byron

**An early-morning walk is a
blessing for the whole day.**

—Henry David Thoreau

You wonder if a fish goes home at night
and exaggerates the size of the bait it stole.

—Bob Hope, Comedian

**The man on top of the mountain
didn't fall there.**

—Vince Lombardi Jr., Football Legend

There is a silence in the imminence of
animals and also in the echo of their noise.

—Peter Matthiessen, *Sand Rivers*

Winter is nature's way of saying, "Up yours."

—ROBERT BYRNE, AMERICAN AUTHOR

There are nights when the wolves are
silent and only the moon howls.

—GEORGE CARLIN, COMEDIAN

The only reason I ever played golf in the first
place was so I could afford to hunt and fish.

—SAM SNEAD, PROFESSIONAL GOLFER

Get drunk by drinking the magical
beauty and tranquil tonic of nature;
get lost in the wilderness.

—DEBASISH MRIDHA, PHYSICIAN & PHILOSOPHER

Embrace the detours.

—KEVIN CHARBONNEAU

Live in the sunshine, swim the
sea, drink the wild air.

—RALPH WALDO EMERSON

**The perils of duck hunting are
great—especially for the duck.**

—WALTER CRONKITE, AMERICAN BROADCAST JOURNALIST

Architects cannot teach nature anything.

—MARK TWAIN

Whenever man comes up with a
better mousetrap, nature immediately
comes up with a better mouse.

—JAMES CARSWELL, SCOTTISH RAILWAY ENGINEER

ACKNOWLEDGMENTS

Thanks to FalconGuides editor, Evan Helmlinger, who entrusted me with this project, my first for Falcon. I'd also like to thank my adventurous and fun-loving girlfriends, my husband who shares a love for the outdoors, my kids who eventually will (I hope), my dad who ignited my love for skiing, my ever-loving mother, and my brother, who I followed out West. And mostly, thanks to all of the writers and adventurers quoted in these pages for sharing their experiences and putting it all so eloquently.

ABOUT THE EDITOR

Corinne Gaffner Garcia has been a writer and editor for close to two decades. She has written extensively for national and regional publications on topics ranging from outdoor adventure (*Women's Adventure, Women's Health, USA Today Travel, Northwest Travel, Via-AAA Magazine*) to parenting (*Parents, Fit Pregnancy*), architecture and homes (*Country Living, Martha Stewart Living*), and general lifestyle (*Marie Claire, Christian Science Monitor*). She is currently the editor in chief for *Big Sky Journal*, a magazine that covers life in the Northern Rockies, and the managing editor for *Western Art & Architecture* magazine. Corinne lives in Bozeman, Montana.